MW01505650

In the Footsteps of
of
Martin Luther

Andy Kuo

"In the Footsteps of ..." Reformation Series

Luke Publishing
Richmond BC Canada

Library and Archives Canada Cataloguing in Publication

Kuo, Andy, author
    In the footsteps of Martin Luther / Andy Kuo.

("In the footsteps of ..." Reformation series)
Includes bibliographical references.
ISBN 978-0-9958266-3-2 (softcover)

    1. Luther, Martin, 1483-1546--Homes and haunts--Germany--Guidebooks. 2. Historic sites--Germany--Guidebooks. 3. Germany--Guidebooks. I. Title. II. Series: Kuo, Andy. "In the footsteps of ..." Reformation series.

BR327.K86 2017   284.1092   C2016-907859-0

A catalogue record for this book is available from Library and Archives Canada

Books in the Series

About the Author

Andy Kuo is an ordained minister of the Presbyterian Church in Canada. His research interests include church history and theology. In his leisure time, he enjoys traveling to historical places.

Dedicated to my wife Julie and my parents.

Front Cover Photo: Night scene in Wittenberg (author's own photo).

Back Cover Photo: Street of Erfurt (author's own photo).

Contents

Preface

M artin Luther, the renowned sixteenth-century reformer, was an ordinary man who accomplished extraordinary things because he believed that God's living Word could change people's lives.

Although he was originally destined to pursue a career in law under his father's arrangement, Luther's life took a significant turn in 1505, when he encountered an awful thunderstorm during his return to Erfurt, Germany, after a trip to his home in Mansfeld. Frightened for his life and of God's judgment, he committed himself to becoming a monk. At the Augustinian monastery in Erfurt, Luther devoted himself to daily prayers, meditations, and study. However, he did not find peace in these strict disciplines and instead became increasingly concerned about his sins.

In 1511, Luther accepted a faculty position at the University of Wittenberg. While preparing a lecture on Paul's letter to the Romans, he made the astounding discovery that God's justice was not a product of human action but a gift received through faith. God's living Word set him free, and at last, his concerns regarding sin and condemnation faded away. When the Catholic Church's renewed campaign of selling indulgences swept through Germany, Luther could not keep quiet anymore. In 1517, he wrote the Ninety-Five Theses, criticizing the overall corruption of the Catholic Church and, specifically, the selling of indulgences, and he nailed it to the door of Castle Church in Wittenberg. The disputation gained immediate popularity and widespread support.

In 1522, Emperor Charles V summoned Luther to attend the Diet of Worms, where the reformer made the following famous statement:

"Unless I am convinced otherwise by evidence from Scripture or incontestable arguments, I remain bound by the Scripture I have put forward. As long as my conscience is captive to the Word of God, I neither can nor will recant, since it is neither safe nor right to act against conscience. God help me. Amen."[1] Afterward, Elector Frederick the Wise—afraid for Luther's life—arranged for him to hide in Wartburg Castle in Eisenach, where Luther spent his time translating the New Testament into German from Greek. He did not return to Wittenberg until the following year.

In 1525, Luther married Katharina von Bora, who had escaped from her convent two years earlier. During their marriage, they had six children. Luther continued his efforts to reform the Church by establishing guidelines and regulations; by composing an order of service in German, known as the German Mass; by writing catechisms, hymns, and tracts; and by continuing to translate the Bible. He continued to labor in Wittenberg until his death in 1546.

In this biographical guided tour, I will take you on a journey through key moments of Martin Luther's life so that you can discover his faith and follow in his footsteps to the places where he traveled. The book is divided into nine chapters, which signify important stages in Luther's life. Each chapter contains a description of that particular stage, and at the end of each chapter, a travel section will introduce you to the cities and sites where Luther traveled at that particular time. Moreover, each travel section will include illustrations of the sites where the principal events of Martin Luther's life took place.

I sincerely hope that this book helps you to not only understand the life of the renowned sixteenth-century reformer, but also follow him to the many places he visited and—more importantly—gain some insight into how his faith shaped him and the people around him.

Andy Kuo

Toronto, Canada

---

1 Martin Luther, *Luther's Works*, ed. Helmut T Lehmann and Jaroslav Pelikan (Philadelphia; St. Louis, Mo.: Fortress Press ; Concordia Pub. House, 2002), 32:112-113.

Timeline

Road to Reformation

1483	Martin Luther was born in Eisleben.
1484	Moved to Mansfeld with his parents.
1497	Attended school in Magdeburg.
1498	Moved to Eisenach to study.
1501	Attended university at Erfurt.
1502	Completed requirements for his bachelor of arts degree.
1505	Obtained his master's degree. Encountered a storm, during which he vowed to become a monk. Joined the Augustinian Order in Erfurt.
1507	Was ordained to the priesthood and celebrated his first Mass.
1511	Accepted a teaching position at the University of Wittenberg and moved to Wittenberg.
1517	Published the Ninety-Five Theses.
1518	Attended the Heidelberg Disputation in Heidelberg. Met Cardinal Cajetan in Augsburg and was ordered to recant. Compiled the *Appellation to the Pope*.
1519	Debated with John Eck at the Leipzig Disputation.

1520	Completed the tracts *To the Christian Nobility of the German Nation, On the Babylonian Captivity,* and *On the Freedom of a Christian.*
	Burned the papal edict that demanded he recant, called *Exsurge Domine.*
1521	Was excommunicated by Pope Leo X.
	Appeared at the Diet of Worms.
1521–22	Was taken to Wartburg Castle.
	Began translating the New Testament into German.

Organizing the Church

1522	Returned to Wittenberg.
	Published the New Testament translation.
1525	The end of the Peasants' War.
	Married Katharina von Bora.
1526	Published the order of service *German Mass.*
ca. 1527–29	Wrote the hymn "A Mighty Fortress Is Our God."
1529	Attended the Marburg Colloquy.
1530	Spent six months in Coburg while the imperial diet was held in Augsburg.
	The Augsburg Confession was presented to Emperor Charles V.
1534	Published his completed translations of the Old Testament and the New Testament.
1536	The Wittenberg Concord was signed by Lutheran and Protestant leaders from southwestern Germany.
1537	Presented the Articles of Faith at the convention of the Schmalkaldic League.
1546	Traveled to Eisleben to settle a dispute over the family business.
	Died in Eisleben.

Luther's Europe
Modified from the original work by Joostik / CC BY-SA 3.0.

Chapter 1: Childhood in Mansfeld

Martin Luther was born in Eisleben on November 10, 1483.[2] He was baptized on November 11 and named after St Martin, the saint of that day. Luther's father, Hans Luder[3], came from Möhra, a town in Thüringen. Hans was the eldest son of peasant parents. Because the mining business was booming, he went to Eisenach, where he met Luther's mother-to-be, Margaret Lindemann; they were betrothed in 1479. Possibly with the help of Margaret's uncle, Anthonius Lindemann—a successful smelter-master in Eisleben as well as the highest-ranking official in the county of Mansfeld—Hans was able to lease copper mines and set up a smelting business.[4]

Less than one year after Martin Luther's birth, he moved with his family to Mansfeld, where he lived until he was sent to school in Magdeburg, the largest city in Saxony, in 1497. Luther probably had eight siblings, but only four survived to adulthood. This was not uncommon, as only about half of the children born in that era lived long enough to become adults.

Having a successful mining business, Hans quickly climbed the

---

2 The exact year of Luther's birth is uncertain. Luther himself claimed that he was born in 1484. However, his colleague, Philip Melanchthon, in his first biographical sketch, placed Luther's birth in 1483, as Luther's brother told him that was Luther's birth date. Moreover, according to Luther's grave marker, he was born in December 1482. This book uses the most widely accepted date of November 10, 1483. For more information, see Scott H. Hendrix, *Martin Luther: Visionary Reformer* (New Haven: Yale University Press, 2015), 17–18.

3 Luther's last name was originally Luder. He changed his last name later in life.

4 Lyndal Roper, *Martin Luther: Renegade and Prophet*, 2016, 18.

social ladder in Mansfeld. He was selected as a representative of the citizenry and also became a member of the brotherhoods of St Anna and St George, both lay religious organizations.

Hans's thriving mining business also guaranteed a comfortable life for the Luther family during Martin's youth. Luther was always grateful to his parents. His father made all the necessary sacrifices to finance his education, and his mother loved him dearly—though in his day, that meant she would discipline him. Later on, Luther shared with his friends and colleagues that his mother had once caught him stealing a single nut, and she had whipped him until he bled.[5] He had found it difficult to accept at the time, but he knew that his mother had meant "heartily well." After all, it was the norm for parents to discipline their children in this manner in his time.

When Luther was around five years old, he started attending Mansfeld's Trivial School. Located next to the Church of St George, the school taught exactly three subjects: grammar, logic, and rhetoric.[6] There Luther studied Latin grammar from the books of Aelius Donatus, read the moral maxims of Cato, and learned the fables of Aesop. He enjoyed them all so much that he later praised them: "After the Bible, the writings of Cato and Aesop are in my judgment the best, better than the mangled opinions of the philosophers and jurists, just as Donatus is the best grammarian."[7]

***

In the first travel section, we will visit the beautiful mining town of Mansfeld, where Martin Luther spent his youth. You will find illustrations of the house in which he lived as a child, the school he attended, and the lovely church where his siblings were baptized. The town of Eisleben, where Luther was born, I will introduce in the final chapter, as it was also where he spent his last days.

---

5 Luther, *Luther's Works*, 54:234-35.
6 Hendrix, *Martin Luther*, 21.
7 Luther, *Luther's Works*, 54:211.

Travel: Mansfeld

Mansfeld was a thriving mining town in Martin Luther's time. In 1500, the town had a population of two to three thousand citizens. The mining industry boom allowed funding for public services, including five hospitals to care for the poor, houses for the sick, and a Latin school for boys.[8] Luther was proud of his roots. He would always say he was from Mansfeld. In fact, in the matriculation book at the University of Erfurt, he referred to himself as "Martin Luther from Mansfeld."[9]

Old town of Mansfeld, view from the castle
© Franzfoto / CC BY-SA 3.0.

8 Roper, *Martin Luther*, 19.
9 The Latin is *Martinus ludher ex mansfelt.* Quoted in Robert Kolb, Irene Dingel, and Lubomir Batka, eds., *The Oxford Handbook of Martin Luther's Theology*, First edition, Oxford Handbooks (Oxford ; New York, NY: Oxford University Press, 2014), 7.

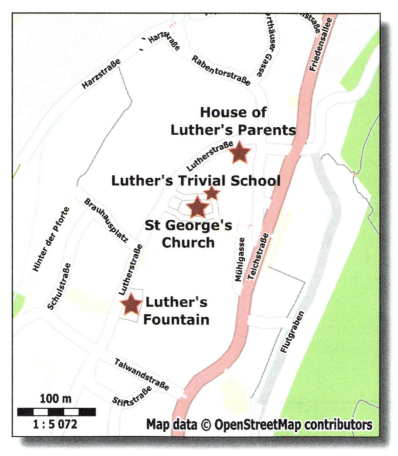

Map of Mansfeld

House of Luther's Parents (*Luthers Elternhaus*)

The Luther family moved to Mansfeld from Eisleben in 1484, and they likely bought this house soon after. The only certain record of Hans having owned the house is found in the town's record from 1507; it indicates that he had already been making mortgage payments on the house for years.[10] We also know that when he became a representative of the citizenry in 1492, the prerequisite for doing so was owning a house. Therefore, it is likely that Luther stayed in this house for the

10 Roper, *Martin Luther*, 19.

duration of his childhood. After Hans's death in 1530, Luther's younger brother, Jacob, inherited the house and their father's business. The Luther family continued to own this house until 1578.

Thanks to recent archaeological discoveries, historians were able to reconstruct the Luthers' way of life at Martin's time. The discovery of animal and fish bones suggests how well the family ate, while the plates and ceramic objects, though not luxurious items, suggested how well the family lived. Children's toys—such as marbles, which Martin and his siblings likely played with—were also found.[11] In addition, these archaeological digs suggested that the property of the house was twice as large as people had originally thought, as it also included a barn and stables for horses as well as a wide entrance for horse-drawn carts to pass through.

A new museum, completed in 2014, now stands opposite the house, on the other side of the road. It presents the Luther family's accounts of Mansfeld as well as their overall relations with the town and church, information on Martin's school years in Mansfeld, and the latest archaeological findings.

House of Luther's Parents
© Tim1900 / CC BY-SA 4.0.

11 Harald Meller et al., eds., *Fundsache Luther: Archäologen auf den Spuren des Reformators ; [Begleitband zur Landesausstellung "Fundsache Luther - Archäologen auf den Spuren des Reformators" im Landesmuseum für Vorgeschichte Halle (Saale) vom 31. Oktober 2008 bis 26. April 2009]* (Stuttgart: Theiss, 2008), 165.

St George's Church

Named after the patron saint of Mansfeld, the Church of St George was built in the thirteenth century and is located in the middle of this former medieval town. When Luther was a teenager, the church burned down when the fire used to heat it was mishandled, but it was reconstructed from 1497 to 1502. The altars, altarpieces, and bells that were consecrated during Luther's lifetime still exist today.

St George's Church (middle)
© Dguendel / CC BY-SA 4.0.

St George's Church was indisputably important to the Luthers. It was the church that Martin and his family attended and in which many of his siblings were possibly baptized. Its worship services likely shaped his sense of sacredness and liturgical practices. Indeed, Luther not only sang in the church choir but probably also served as an altar boy.[12] Although construction of the new building began the same year as his departure to Magdeburg, Luther often visited St George's Church, both during his studies and later in life.

---

12 "St. George's Church, Mansfeld," accessed September 28, 2016, http://www.welterbe-luther.de/en/extension-application/st-georges-church-mansfeld.

Current highlights include the only full portrait of Martin Luther in regalia still in existence as well as the painting *Resurrection of Christ* by Lucas Cranach the Elder, who was Luther's close friend in Wittenberg.

Luther's Fountain (*Lutherbrunnen*)

Located at Luther Place (Lutherplatz), this beautiful fountain was built in 1913. The monument portrays three important moments in Martin Luther's life, which can be seen on each of its three sides. The first side depicts the young Luther, who bid farewell to Mansfeld in 1497. The German inscription reads *Hinaus in die Welt*, which translates to "Out into the World." The second side reveals Luther nailing the Ninety-Five Theses to the door of Castle Church in Wittenberg. The inscription reads *Hinein in den Kampf*, which translates to "Into the Battle." The third side pictures Luther's presence at the Diet of Worms. The inscription reads *Hindurch zum Sieg*, which translates to "Through to Victory."

Luther's Fountain
© Dguendel / CC BY-SA 3.0.

Luther's Trivial School (*Luthers Schule*)

In 1488, Luther was enrolled in Mansfeld's trivial school, located north of the Church of St George. He studied there until 1497. Besides studying grammar, logic, and rhetoric, he and the other children learned to recite the creed, the Hail Mary, and various passages from the Latin Bible. Incidentally, in Luther's time, discipline was administered through corporal punishment. He recalled in 1524 that he was "once beaten fifteen times one after another in one morning."[13] Today, the school stands beside the town hall while the former school houses the town's tourist office. Every year, on the first Saturday after Easter, Mansfeld celebrates Luther's first day of school.

The current school (left) beside the town hall (center)
© Pomfuttage / CC BY-SA 3.0.

---

13 Quoted in Roper, *Martin Luther*, 36.

Chapter 2: Teenage Years

Magdeburg

In 1497, when Martin Luther was about fourteen, his parents sent him to Magdeburg to pursue further studies. He traveled with Hans Reinicke, another boy from Mansfeld. Precisely where Luther attended school in Magdeburg remains uncertain, but it has been said that his schooling was related to the Brethren of the Common Life, which is closely associated with the cathedral.[14] Therefore, his teachers would have primarily been priests or bishops from the cathedral. Martin and Hans would later take different paths in life. Reinicke inherited his father's business and became one of the wealthiest mine owners in Mansfeld. Luther, on the other hand, went on to study at the University of Erfurt before he became a monk and professor. Despite their differences, the two of them remained good friends throughout their lives.

Eisenach

In 1498, after spending only one year in Magdeburg, Luther moved to Eisenach—a smaller town of three or four thousand citizens—to continue his studies. This choice was likely influenced by his mother, Margaret Lindemann, who came from Eisenach, where the Lindemann family was prominent. As a matter of fact, many of Luther's relatives were university graduates with professions as doctors, academics, administrators, and lawyers.[15] This constructive atmosphere likely inspired Luther to pursue studies at university later. While in Eisenach, Luther

---

14 Hendrix, *Martin Luther*, 23.
15 Roper, *Martin Luther*, 38–39.

may have lived with Conrad Cotta's family.[16] Conrad's father-in-law was Heinrich Schalbe, who happened to be both his mother's relative and the mayor of Eisenach from 1495 to 1499.

Luther studied in Eisenach for three years; the school curriculum included advanced grammar, logic, and rhetoric. Since it was associated with St George's Church, the students also served and participated in the church events. Luther thereby developed his musical skills, including a decent tenor voice and an overall understanding of musical theory.[17] As a classmate later recalled, by the time Luther entered university, he was already "a learned musician and philosopher."[18] His talents certainly proved helpful during the Reformation, as he arranged tunes and wrote hymns in order to reform the liturgy.

While in Eisenach, Luther immersed himself in its spiritual culture. Despite its small population, the town had three parish churches, seven monasteries, and nine chapels. Each church had multiple altars— St Mary's alone had twenty-three altars, and St George's had eighteen. It was estimated that one in every ten residents was either a priest or a monk.[19] Like Mansfeld, the town's patron saint was St George, who had—according to legend—slain a dragon. Unlike Mansfeld, Eisenach was counterbalanced by another patron saint: St Elizabeth, who looked after the town's minorities. Luther was deeply touched by her story. When other saints came under attack during the Reformation, he still spoke of this one with reverence.[20] In fact, he named his first daughter Elisabeth.

Luther and other pupils from the school sometimes went door to door, singing for bread, as was the tradition in Eisenach.[21] They were often invited to the home of John Braun, a local priest who served at St Mary's, for evenings of music and discussion.[22] Luther developed a

---

16 Martin Brecht, *Martin Luther: His Road to Reformation, 1483-1521*, 1st pbk. ed (Minneapolis: Fortress Press, 1993), 18.
17 Hendrix, *Martin Luther*, 24.
18 Quoted in Ibid.
19 Ibid.
20 Roper, *Martin Luther*, 40.
21 Luther, *Luther's Works*, 46:250.
22 Hendrix, *Martin Luther*, 25.

close friendship with this man that lasted for many years. His overall experience in Eisenach was very positive, and he later described it as his "beloved town."[23]

***

In the travel section that follows, we will visit the beautiful Gothic cathedral in Magdeburg. After that, we will visit Luther's beloved town of Eisenach to see the museum house where he lived as a teenager, the gorgeous church where he joined the choir, and Wartburg Castle—which perches over the town—where Luther hid while he translated the Bible.

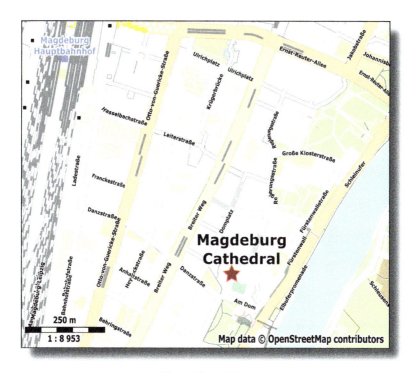

Map of Magdeburg

---

23 Quoted in Ibid., 24.

Travel: Magdeburg and Eisenach

MAGDEBURG

Situated on the picturesque Elbe River, Magdeburg is the capital of the state of Saxony-Anhalt in east-central Germany. The city was founded as a small trading settlement in 805 and went on to become an important city in medieval times. In 1497, fourteen-year-old Martin Luther studied here before moving on to Eisenach. Although his stay in Magdeburg was brief, he visited the city once after he became an Augustinian monk and again after he became a well-known reformer.

Magdeburg, with the cathedral dominating its skyline

Magdeburg Cathedral

Magdeburg Cathedral was the first Gothic cathedral built in all of Germany and one of the tallest in eastern Germany. Its construction was started in 1209 but completed no less than three centuries later. When Luther arrived in Magdeburg in 1497, the steeple was only half finished. Once completed, the cathedral dominated the skyline of Magdeburg, and it does to this day. It is worth noting that while Luther lived there, the archbishop was Ernest II of Saxony, brother of electors Frederick the Wise and John the Steadfast. The two electors later protected and supported Luther during the Reformation.

EISENACH

Located in western Thuringia, the scenic town of Eisenach has a current population of around 42,000. In the thirteenth century, it was the capital of Thuringia. Luther came here in 1498 to study until his departure for university in 1501. The town also claims Johann Sebastian Bach as its own. That renowned German conductor and musician was indeed born in Eisenach and baptized in St George's Church.

A view of Eisenach
© Westerdam / CC BY-SA 4.0.

13

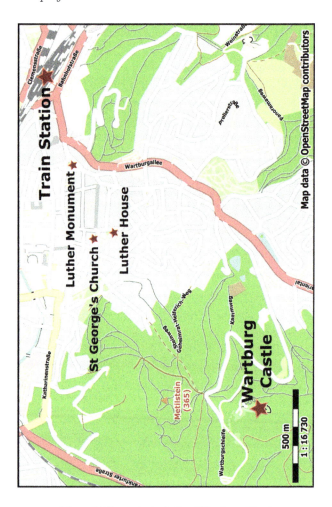

Map of Eisenach, including Wartburg Castle

Luther House (*Lutherhaus*)

This half-timbered house is one of the oldest of its kind in Thuringia. It is believed that Luther lived here from 1498 to 1501. Over the past five centuries, the house has been put to different uses by various owners. In 1956, however, it was dedicated as the Luther House Museum. The museum was recently renovated and reopened on September 26, 2015. Exhibitions include Luther's translation of the Bible, some of

Lucas Cranach the Elder's artwork, and even the baptismal record of Johann Sebastian Bach.

Luther House

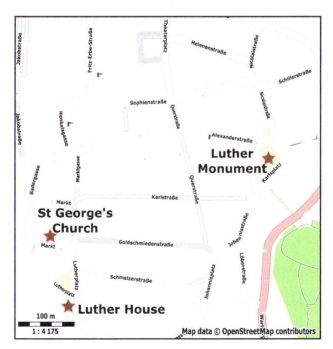

Map of Eisenach's old town

Luther Monument (*Lutherdenkmal*)

Martin Luther Monument
© J.-H. Janßen / CC BY-SA 4.0.

Located in Karlsplatz, the oldest marketplace in Eisenach, is sculptor Adolf von Donndorf's Martin Luther Monument. It was dedicated on May 4, 1895, on the 374th anniversary of Luther's arrival at Wartburg Castle. The statue depicts Luther holding a Bible in his hand.

Below the statue, on each of the monument's four sides, reliefs display specific scenes from Luther's life in Eisenach. The west relief shows Luther when he first came to the city, caroling with fellow students and being welcomed by Ursula Cotta—the daughter of Heinrich Schalbe, who was mayor at that time. The south relief illustrates Luther's room at Wartburg Castle, where he spent his time translating the Bible. The eastern relief presents a bearded Luther, disguised as "Junker Jörg." Finally, the north relief displays the title of Luther's most famous hymn, "A Mighty Fortress Is Our God."

St George's Church (*Georgenkirche*)

Named after the town's patron saint, St George's Church was founded in 1180. It was here that Luther participated in the choir and thus developed his musical talents. Moreover, when he was on his way to and from the Diet of Worms, Luther returned to this church to preach.

16

On its north wall, a large painting commemorates the Reformation with its depiction of Martin Luther, the Bohemian reformer Jan Hus, and the Augsburg Confession. The original baptismal font that was used in 1685 to baptize Johann Sebastian Bach likewise remains at the church and is still well-preserved today.

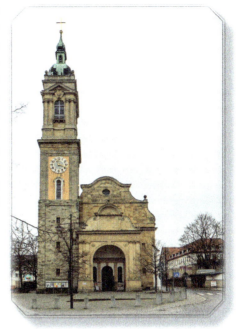

St George's Church
© NoRud / CC BY-SA 4.0.

Wartburg Castle

Perched over the town of Eisenach is the magnificent Wartburg Castle, which was founded around 1067. In medieval times, it served as the residence of the counts who ruled the region. In the early thirteenth century, the castle became home to St Elizabeth, the daughter of Andrew II of Hungary, who had been sent to marry Ludwig IV of Thuringia and whose practice of helping the town's needy was well remembered by its people. In May 1521, Luther came to Wartburg Castle under the arrangement of the elector Frederick the Wise. One of the major works that Luther completed here was his translation of the New Testament from Greek to German.

Wartburg Castle
© JörgGehlmann / CC BY-SA 4.0.

Today, the museum within Wartburg Castle offers information on St Elizabeth's life and displays portraits of Martin Luther and his parents. The Luther Room (Lutherstube), where Luther spent his time, is located along the gallery, through the low arches.

Luther Room
© J.-H. Janßen / CC BY-SA 4.0.

Chapter 3: Years in Erfurt

University Years

At the age of eighteen, Martin Luther traveled thirty-five miles to study law at the University of Erfurt. He likely left Eisenach in April 1501 to make it in time for the summer semester.[24] As he made his way through the pleasant springtime weather, he no doubt took notice of the tree branches sprouting all around him. At that time, Luther's future was just as hopeful as that springtime sight. Erfurt, the capital of Thuringia, was even larger than Eisenach, with a population of about nineteen thousand. Known for its innumerable religious institutions, the city was nicknamed "Rome of the North." It also hosted a top-level university, a college of liberal arts, three professional schools, and theological programs for three monastic orders.

At university, students wore distinctive garb and lodged in a number of different residential colleges. Luther likely lived in at least two of them. Luther's relative, Dietrich Lindemann, recalled from a visit that Martin lived in the residence of St George; however, other evidence indicates that he may have stayed in the larger Amplonian College.[25] School life was regulated under a strict set of rules.[26] Students had to wake up at four o'clock in the morning and go to bed at eight o'clock in the evening. Attendance at Mass was also monitored. Professors and their associates often provided oversight to students in their daily living. Though the rules may have been harsh, students were obviously able to find ways around them. In fact, when Luther looked back on his

24 Ibid., 27.
25 Ibid.
26 Ibid., 29.

university days thirty years later, he referred to the town as "a whorehouse and beer house; these two lessons are what students got from that gymnasium."[27] Luther may have enjoyed drinking beer, but there is nothing to suggest that he misbehaved during that time.

In 1502, Luther graduated with mediocre grades, ranking thirtieth among fifty-seven graduates.[28] Right after graduation, he continued to study toward a master's degree, which only a handful of his fellow students wished to pursue. At this point, he began to show signs of becoming a bright academic scholar. Indeed, when Luther passed his master's exam in 1505, he ranked second among seventeen graduates.

The University of Erfurt also produced scholars like George Spalatin, John Lang, and Justus Jonas, who all went on to support the Reformation. Though Luther and Spalatin never met while they studied at Erfurt, Spalatin later became Luther's liaison at the court of Elector Frederick in Wittenberg. He furthermore helped to secure protection for Luther against the Catholic Church, whose authorities wanted him removed. Lang joined the Augustinian Order a year after Luther. When they were sent to Wittenberg, Lang taught Greek there. Though Jonas was much younger than both Luther and Lang, he nonetheless became Luther's colleague in Wittenberg and accompanied him to many important events, including the Diet of Worms; he was even present for the final days of Luther's life.

An Augustinian Monk

In 1505 a plague struck Erfurt, and disease killed three of Luther's friends. At that time, no one knew how or why this happened; they only had a general sense that it was God passing judgment on their sins. This way of thinking led Luther to one of the most critical turning points in his life. On July 2, 1505, he was returning to Erfurt on horseback after a trip home to Mansfeld when he encountered a terrible thunderstorm near Stotternheim. Terrified that it could be the devil causing the storm, Luther called on St Anna—the patron saint of miners—for help. He shouted, "Help, St Anna! I will become a monk!"[29]

---

27 Quoted in Brecht, *Martin Luther*, 30; Roper, *Martin Luther*, 44.
28 Brecht, *Martin Luther*, 33.
29 Quoted in Ibid., 48.

When he finally got to Erfurt, Luther kept his vow. He organized a farewell party for his classmates and friends, a lavish meal with music and other entertainment. At the party, he announced his decision: "Today you see me and never again!"[30] His friends were shocked, and some of them tried to dissuade him, without success. After the party, Luther knocked at the door of the Augustinian monastery in Erfurt.

Luther's decision was a terrible blow to his father, who had invested heavily in his son's education. Martin did not even present his resolution in person but rather in a simple letter. Hans remained bitter about it for years afterward. As a matter of fact, at the first Mass that Luther conducted after his ordination, he asked whether his father would accept his decision; Hans replied, in front of everyone, "Let us hope that your vow was not an illusion," followed by, "Have you not heard that parents are to be obeyed?"[31]

Monastic life involved strict discipline. Luther's hair was shaved to conform with the distinctive tonsure of the Augustinian Order.[32] In addition, he was dressed in the Augustinian habit, consisting of "a short woolen tunic covered by a long black cowl or gown and topped by a hood; leather straps for a belt; and finally the scapula, a shoulder-length white collar with an opening for his head."[33] In the monastery, the day was divided so that prayers could be said throughout. Their sleep was also divided, so that the monks could wake up and say morning prayers. A mass was said each day, and psalms were sung seven times a day, which resulted in the singing of 150 psalms a week. The monks ate two meals a day while they listened to Scripture read aloud. Other times were allocated to silence, study, instruction, confession, and more. After a year, Luther was assigned a cell for study and prayer, a stall in the chancel for worship, and a place in the common dormitory to sleep. Such strict discipline left a deep mark on his health. Indeed, Luther later stated, "If I hadn't done it, I would be healthier and stronger."[34]

---

30 Quoted in Roper, *Martin Luther*, 47.
31 Hendrix, *Martin Luther*, 38.
32 Brecht, *Martin Luther*, 63–70.
33 Hendrix, *Martin Luther*, 35.
34 Quoted in Roper, *Martin Luther*, 57.

During Luther's time in the monastery, he became increasingly concerned about his inability to please God and achieve salvation. Even though he confessed his sins earnestly for several hours each day, he could find no assurance that God was forgiving him. He finally appealed to his confessors for help, but they only said that he was too strict in counting his sins. Luther then went to the early church fathers, medieval theologians, and the Bible to seek the answers he wanted, but it was to no avail. He continued to struggle.

While at the monastery, Luther also prepared for a career in the priesthood. He was ordained in the chapel of St Kilian at Erfurt Cathedral in April 1507. As an ordained priest, Luther was obligated to perform the Mass; however, he found himself unworthy to perform such a holy task before God and would not endure it for even an hour without confessing his sins.[35] In 1508, Luther was assigned a temporary position at the University of Wittenberg, a newly funded university in need of faculty. He lectured there for a year while he completed the first part of his doctoral studies, after which he returned to Erfurt to continue his education.

Trip to Rome

Around this time, Luther traveled to Rome with another Augustinian monk (whose name is unknown) to try to settle a matter within the Augustinian Order.[36] It was the longest journey he ever took and the only trip he ever made outside Germany. Covering about nine hundred miles, the two monks crossed the Alps through the Septimer Pass.[37] When they arrived in Italy, they traveled to Rome via Milan and Florence. It took them two full months to reach the capital of the Roman Catholic Church. When Luther and his companion finally did turn up, Raphael—the famous Renaissance artist—was painting the pope's private apartment while Michelangelo—another famous Renaissance artist—was working on the ceiling of the Sistine Chapel. The new St Peter's Basilica was still in its design stage; the old one was neverthe-

---

35 Brecht, *Martin Luther*, 72.
36 Scholars differ on which year Luther traveled to Rome. Hendrix stated that it was in 1511 while Brecht placed the year as 1510. If it was 1511, he would have traveled to Rome after he settled in Wittenberg. See Hendrix, *Martin Luther*, 6.
37 Brecht, *Martin Luther*, 100.

less magnificent. Rome was home not only to St Peter's and the pope but also to the saints and martyrs who endured. Every year, tens of thousands of pilgrims traveled to the city to draw closer to God. Even though Rome was the "holy city" of the West, Luther discovered that the Church had become a secular institution. He was shocked to see how irreverently the Roman priests were performing the Mass; they would say the Mass so quickly that seven of them could be completed within an hour.[38] On one of his visits to see the relics, Luther remembered that one cleric had shoved him out and rushed him through.[39]

***

In the travel section that follows, we will visit the medieval town of Erfurt. I will introduce you to various sites, including the ancient university campus where Luther studied, the magnificent cathedral where he was ordained into the priesthood, and the Augustinian monastery where he spent many years as a monk before moving to Wittenberg.

---

38 Ibid., 102.
39 Roper, *Martin Luther*, 63.

Travel: Erfurt

L ocated in the center of modern-day Germany, Erfurt is the capital city of the state of Thuringia. Its archaic townscape even now remains intact, making it a charming place to visit. The city is surrounded by bountiful fields, which led Luther to call it a "very fertile Bethlehem."[40] In medieval times, Erfurt became a prosperous commercial center because it stood at the intersection of trade routes that connected Western and Eastern Europe. Every year, the city celebrates Martin Luther's birthday on November 10.

Erfurt as viewed from the castle
Photography by the author

---

40 Hendrix, *Martin Luther*, 28.

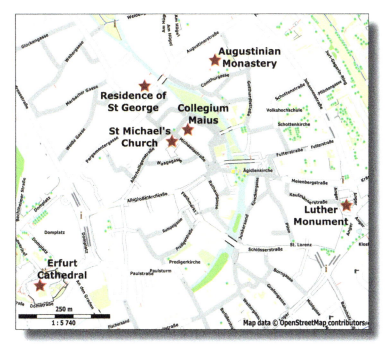

Map of Erfurt

University of Erfurt

Founded in 1379, the University of Erfurt is the oldest public university in Germany. In Martin Luther's time, it became a hotbed for the Renaissance humanism that would later help to foster the Reformation. Another famous alumnus was Johannes Gutenberg, who went on to introduce the movable-type printing press to all of Europe. The university was closed in 1816 and did not reopen until 1994, after the reunification of Germany. The core district from Luther's time is located around the corridor of *Michaelisstrasse* street.

Collegium Maius

Located on *Michaelisstrasse*, the *Collegium Maius* was the first and principal building at the University of Erfurt. Unfortunately, it was mostly destroyed during World War II. Its reconstruction was completed

25

in 1999. Today, the building houses Central Germany's Evangelical Church.

Collegium Maius
Photograph by the author

Residence of St George (Georgenburse)

Now an important center for discussion and education, the Residence of St George was one of two residences where Luther lived during his stay at Erfurt. His day started and ended relatively early, and he ate only two meals a day. Today, the building offers accommodation to pilgrims.

Residence of St George

St Michael's Church (Michaeliskirche)

St Michael's Church was the University of Erfurt's church. After the city had embraced the Reformation, Luther visited Erfurt and preached at St Michael's on October 21, 1522. John Lang, Luther's friend and fellow reformer, started to preach there in 1530 and was buried there in 1548.

St Michael's Church
Photograph by the author

Erfurt Cathedral

Located on the small hill in Cathedral Square (*Domplatz*) are two churches whose entrances face each other—Erfurt Cathedral on the left and St Severus Church on the right. Based on the foundation of the original church that stood there before—which St Boniface erected in the eighth century—Erfurt Cathedral was built in the fourteenth century. After a fire in the fifteenth century, it was rebuilt to be larger. It was here, in the chapel of St Kilian, that Martin Luther was ordained into the priesthood in April 1507.

27

Erfurt Cathedral (left) and St Severus Church (right)
Photograph by the author

Augustinian Monastery and Church
(Augustinerkloster und Augustinerkirche)

Built around 1300, this Augustinian monastery was where Martin Luther joined the Augustinian Order on July 17, 1505. He lived here for several years before he moved on to Wittenberg in 1511. Life in the monastery was very simple, as the Augustinians followed the principles of *ora et labora* ("pray and work"). The exact reason why Luther chose the Augustinian Order remains uncertain, though it was likely due to the monastery's wealth of academic resources as compared to those of the Dominicans and the Franciscans. Besides, many members of the monastery were also faculty at the university.

During World War II, a bomb destroyed the library. It was a tragic event, as the blast hit several hundred of the monastery's residents in hiding, resulting in 267 casualties. The site of the original library now houses offices and a conference center. Both the church and the cloister are still intact today.

The courtyard of the monastery
Photograph by the author

The Church

The Augustinian church was where Luther worshipped during his stay at the monastery. He and other monks would kneel in front of the altar, or lie on their backs with their arms outstretched, to meditate. After Luther was ordained into the priesthood in 1507, he also performed the Mass here. At the altar lies the tomb of Johannes Zacharias, who encouraged the Church to burn Bohemian reformer Jan Hus at the stake in 1415. Ironically, a century later Luther's meditation at Zacharias's tomb would lead him to the ideas that sparked the Reformation.

The altar at the Augustinian church
Photograph by the author

The Cloister

The cloister contains an exhibition on the history of the Bible as well as a model of a fifteenth-century printing press. A room dedicated to Martin Luther is lined with small cells where the monks would have meditated. Luther's was the cell in the far corner (*Lutherzelle*). It includes the table where Luther used to read and write.

Luther Cell
© Dr. Bernd Gross / CC BY-SA 3.0.

Luther Monument (*Lutherdenkmal*)

Unveiled on October 30, 1889, the Luther Monument shows the reformer Martin Luther holding an open Bible in his left hand. The reliefs on three sides of its base illustrate different stages of his life in Erfurt: Luther as a student with his classmates, his farewell before he entered the monastery, and his festive reception at the University of

Erfurt in April 1521, when he was on his way to Worms. On the front of the base is an inscription taken from Psalm 118:17: "I will not die but live, and will proclaim what the Lord has done."

The location of the statue, in front of Merchant's Church, was chosen because Luther delivered a sermon at the church in 1522 to settle a religious dispute. Merchant's Church was also where Johann Sebastian Bach's parents were married in 1668.

Luther Monument
Photograph by the author

Chapter 4: The Ninety-Five Theses

Confessor Johann von Staupitz

In 1511, Martin Luther returned to Wittenberg, where he had previously lectured from 1508 to 1509. He was to accept a teaching position at the town's newly built Wittenberg University. This time, Luther would make Wittenberg his home for the rest of his life. For this, Luther owed credit to his confessor, Johann von Staupitz.

Staupitz likely met Luther in April 1506. When Luther was going through his internal struggle with God's wrath over his sins, it was Staupitz who continued to remind him that God's love and mercy were greater than God's judgment.[41] The older, and wiser Staupitz saw in Luther a bright young scholar; he even encouraged Luther to take the teaching position at the university and pursue doctoral studies in theology. Luther later recalled a conversation he had had with Staupitz in the courtyard of the monastery at Wittenberg. He had told Staupitz that he had no intention to become a doctor, as he did not know how long he would live. But Staupitz convinced him that God needed clever people, whether on earth or in heaven.[42] Luther accepted this challenge: he went on to Wittenberg in 1511, received his doctorate, and was inducted into the faculty in 1512.

---

41 Brecht, *Martin Luther*, 26.
42 Hendrix, *Martin Luther*, 44.

Wittenberg

Wittenberg was a newly built town. The elector Frederick the Wise had chosen it as his base when he had inherited Saxony in 1486. He had ambitious plans for the town: besides a beautiful castle as his place of residence, he wished to build an internationally renowned university. When Luther arrived in 1511, Wittenberg was a construction site. Castle Church, which was officially called the Church of All Saints, had been completed only two years earlier. Frederick used it to house his collection of relics. In addition, the university buildings were still under construction; the town hall had just been started; and the Augustinian cloister—where Luther likely stayed when he arrived—was still in its initial construction stage, with only one dormitory completed.

Up until 1517, besides the academic work that he had to attend to, Luther was occupied with his monastic duties. In a letter to John Lang, his colleague and friend, he described his life this way: "I could almost occupy two scribes or secretaries. All day long I do nothing but write letters…I have little uninterrupted time for the daily [monastic] hours or for celebrating mass. Beside, I have my own struggles with the flesh, the world, and the devil. See what a lazy man I am!"[43] His monastic duties were not minor. As the provincial vicar, he had to attend to the administrative matters of eleven other cloisters in the province as well as visit them regularly.

The Epistle to the Romans

As a professor, Luther lectured on different books of the Bible. In August 1513, he delivered his first lecture on the Psalms. After that, he chose books from the New Testament. While he was preparing his lectures on Romans, Luther struggled with the meaning of Romans 1:17, where Paul reminds us that God's justice is revealed in the gospel, not in the law. Thus, Luther finally made the discovery that God's justice was a gift received through faith, and not a product of human action as the Church would have him believe. He reflected, "For the justice of God is the cause of salvation…By the justice of God we must not understand the justice by which God is just in himself but the justice

---

43 Luther to John Lang, October 26, 1516. Quoted in Ibid., 45.

by which we are made just by God. This happens through faith in the gospel."[44] This became the basis of the doctrinal statement "justification by faith."

Years later, as he reflected on his discovery, Luther wrote, "I began to understand that God's justice meant that people who were just in God's sight lived by a divine gift. It is the passive justice by which God justifies us through faith, as it is written: 'They who through faith are just shall live' (Habakkuk 2:4). I felt I was altogether born again and had entered paradise through open gates!"[45] It was not an entirely new discovery; the fourth-century theologian Augustine had made a similar claim during his conflict with the Pelagians. Nevertheless, it was an "aha" moment for Luther. Through the Scripture, he had finally uncovered the fountain that quenched his spiritual thirst by resolving his uncertainty about God's salvation.

The Ninety-Five Theses

As 1517 approached, Luther was delivering lectures, preaching at the town church of St Mary, and attending to administrative tasks as the provincial vicar of the Augustinian Order. All of that changed when a Dominican friar named John Tetzel arrived in Jüterbog, a small town northeast of Wittenberg. Tetzel had been selected by Archbishop Albert of Brandenburg to sell indulgences in the archdioceses of Mainz and Magdeburg. An indulgence was an official paper that afforded its owner certain benefits; the practice of trading in these papers became very attractive, as they supposedly spared sinners from punishment for their past and future transgressions and furthermore offered them the release of their loved ones from purgatory. Pope Leo X, quite a spendthrift, was hoping that the selling of indulgences would bring in more funds.

Elector Frederick the Wise declared his territory off limits, but when Tetzel arrived in Jüterbog, just outside of Saxony, many of Frederick's people made the journey to purchase indulgences.[46] After all,

---

44 Luther, *Luther's Works*, 25:151-52.
45 Ibid., 34:337.
46 Brecht, *Martin Luther*, 183.

a trip of twenty-five miles did not compare to the promises that an indulgence could offer. A veteran promoter, Tetzel made despicable claims: "Have mercy upon your dead parents." "Whoever has an indulgence has salvation; anything else is of no avail."[47]

Luther became preoccupied with the selling of indulgences. In February 1517, while preaching at the town church, he urged his congregation to atone for their own sins rather than hope that a piece of paper would spare them any penalties.[48] Luther felt that the practice devalued the importance of penance. He was also concerned that the selling of indulgences brought fear to people, emphasizing God's wrath and diminishing the importance of God's love—that is, Christ's suffering—for God's people.

Feeling that he could no longer keep quiet, Luther prepared a letter to Archbishop Albert on October 31, 1517. In the letter, he humbly asked the archbishop to rescind his instruction to sell indulgences, as it had been issued under the archbishop's name. Luther also attached two documents: his Ninety-Five Theses and an essay on indulgences. In the Ninety-Five Theses, he criticized the selling of indulgences, stating that they provided false security and de-emphasized true contrition. He contested the "necessity" of taking money from poor believers simply to afford the construction of St Peter's Basilica in Rome. And finally, Luther demanded to know why the pope would not free his own followers from purgatory purely out of love, and do so only through indulgences.

On the same day Luther wrote his letter, he nailed the Ninety-Five Theses onto the door of Castle Church (All Saints Church). There were scholarly debates on whether Luther actually posted the document so publicly or whether he intended to have it circulate among a smaller group of people.[49] Even if it was nailed to the door, few would have been able to understand it, as it was written in Latin. Nevertheless, Luther's Ninety-Five Theses prompted a chain reaction that eventually led to reformation throughout Europe. By the end of 1517, they had

---

47 Ibid.
48 Ibid., 183–90.
49 See Hendrix, *Martin Luther*, 61–62.

been printed three times in Leipzig, Nuremberg, and Basel. The original Latin had also been translated into German.

John Tetzel did not receive the Ninety-Five Theses well. In fact, he threatened to "throw that heretic Luther into the fire."[50] In the first half of 1518, he accused Luther of attacking papal authority. John Eck, a prominent professor at Ingolstadt, also considered Luther's theses heretical. In Rome, Silvester Prierias, a Dominican friar and theologian, attacked Luther by declaring the Ninety-Five Theses erroneous.[51]

By the spring of 1518, Luther had realized that the battle ahead was going to be tough, but he refused to give up. He dedicated an extensive document called *Explanations* to the pope, therein explaining that the Ninety-Five Theses were only intended for discussion, not doctrines or dogmas.[52] At that point, Luther was not planning to separate from the Roman Catholic Church; he was merely seeking reform. Perhaps his letter to Staupitz on March 31, 1518, summarized his intentions well: "I teach that people should put their trust in nothing but Jesus Christ alone, not in their prayers, merits, or their own good deeds."[53]

***

In the travel section that follows, we will visit Wittenberg, the birthplace of Luther's Reformation and the town he made his home from 1511 to the end of his life. It was here that he participated in many significant historical events. I will introduce you to Castle Church, where Luther nailed his Ninety-Five Theses, as well as the home of Lucas Cranach the Elder, a famous German artist and friend of Luther's. I will introduce the town's other sites in the travel section of Chapter 7.

---

50 Ibid., 65.
51 Brecht, *Martin Luther*, 209.
52 Luther, *Luther's Works*, 31:83-252.
53 Letter to Staupitz on March 31, 1518. Quoted in Hendrix, *Martin Luther*, 68.

Travel: Wittenberg Part 1

Known as the birthplace of the Protestant Reformation, Wittenberg owes its fame to Martin Luther. The town started off as a small village in the twelfth century and gradually became an important political and cultural center. However, it was not until Frederick the Wise made his residence in Wittenberg, and founded the University of Wittenberg, that the town became truly prosperous.

View of Wittenberg from the bell tower of the Castle Church
© theotherpaul / CC BY-SA 3.0.

Map of Wittenberg

The Castle Church (*Schlosskirche*)

Located at the west end of town, Castle Church is best known for Martin Luther's decision to nail the Ninety-Five Theses to its wooden door on October 31, 1517. The Castle Church constructed under the order of elector Frederick the Wise, beginning in 1489, christened All Saints' Church on January 17, 1503, and was finally completed in 1509.

When Luther first arrived in Wittenberg, it was a brand-new facility. Even though the university used it as both a chapel and auditorium, it was not actually open to the public in Luther's time. The townspeople worshipped at St Mary's, while Castle Church was used only on special occasions. For instance, around the time of All Saints' Day, the elector would open Castle Church to the townspeople, who were invited to come see the vast collection of relics that were housed inside. Incidentally, Frederick the Wise—who was a strong supporter of Luther's—nonetheless remained a devout Roman Catholic all his life.

The Castle Church
© Dr. Avishai Teicher / CC BY-SA 4.0.

The Door

The door where Martin Luther nailed a handwritten copy of his Ninety-Five Theses was in the middle of the church, to the left of its current entrance. The original wooden door no longer exists, as it was destroyed in 1760, during the Seven Years' War. Castle Church was rebuilt in the Romantic style at some point in the nineteenth century. Its door was replaced with a bronze one that had the Ninety-Five Theses engraved in it in Latin. Above the door, a splendid painting depicts the crucified Christ, with Martin Luther and Philipp Melanchthon (Luther's right-hand man) on either side. The skyline of Wittenberg can be seen in the background.

The door where Luther nailed his Ninety-Five Theses
Photograph by the author

The Bell Tower

Standing at 289 feet tall, the Bell Tower—once part of Wittenberg Castle—was also incorporated into the restoration of Castle Church in the late nineteenth century. From the steeple, one can see a spectacular view of Wittenberg and its surroundings. Martin Luther's famous hymn, "A Mighty Fortress Is Our God," has been inscribed on it in large German letters.

Stained-Glass Windows

Toward the front of the nave stands a huge stained-glass window. The upper part of the window includes the beautiful coats of arms of the German cities that switched to Protestantism throughout the Reformation. It was installed in the late nineteenth century. The three lower windows, which depict the medallions of twelve important European Reformation figures, were installed in 1983—on the five hundredth anniversary of Martin Luther's birth.

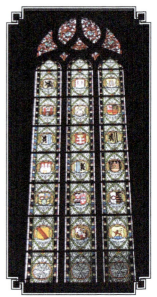

The upper stained-glass window depicting the German cities that joined the Reformation
© Benutzer / CC BY-SA 3.0.

Tomb of Martin Luther

Luther's coffin was buried beside the nave and in front of the pulpit. A Latin epitaph reads, "Here lies the body of Martin Luther, Doctor of Sacred Theology, who died in his hometown Eisleben in the year of our Lord 1546 on the 18th day of February after having lived for 63 years, 2 months and 10 days."

The tombstone of Martin Luther
Photograph by the author

40

Tomb of Philipp Melanchthon

Philipp Melanchthon's coffin was buried similarly but on the opposite side of the nave from Luther's. An epitaph reads, "Here rests the body of the most commendable Philipp Melanchthon, who died on 19 April 1560, in this town after he had lived for 63 years 2 months and 2 days."

Tomb Markers of Frederick the Wise and John the Steadfast

The tomb markers of Frederick the Wise and John the Steadfast—the two electors from Luther's time—are in front and to either side of the high altar. Although Frederick remained a devout Catholic throughout his life, he ensured that Luther—his young and promising professor— received necessary support in key moments. For instance, he made sure that Luther would have a fair hearing at the Diet of Worms in Germany instead of a trial in Rome; he convinced Emperor Charles V to provide Luther safe conduct so that he could attend the Diet; and he hid Luther at Wartburg Castle when his life was in danger.

Frederick's brother, John the Steadfast, succeeded him as elector. Unlike Frederick, John converted to Protestantism; after inheriting his brother's title, he destroyed Frederick's vast collection of relics. He fervently supported Luther's Reformation throughout his life.

Cranach Courtyard (*Cranachhof*)

The former residence of German Renaissance artist Lucas Cranach the Elder (1472–1553) is a Renaissance building with a large courtyard. Inside the courtyard is a statue of Lucas Cranach the Elder sketching, commemorating Germany's famous painter. Cranach the Elder, the official court painter of Frederick the Wise in Luther's time, had a wonderful friendship with Luther. He was the only painter with permission to paint Martin and his family. He and his son, Lucas Cranach the Younger, produced and reproduced more than two thousand Luther portraits. Since he was another enthusiastic supporter of Luther's movement, Cranach the Elder's religious paintings effectively conveyed the theological ideas of the Reformation. Indeed, his artwork made its way into many of Luther's books. Katharina von Bora—who would later become Luther's wife—even lived at Cranach's home when she first came to Wittenberg.

Statue of Lucas Cranach the Elder sketching
Photograph by the author

Chapter 5: Disputations

The Heidelberg Disputation

After Luther posted the Ninety-Five Theses, he found himself attacked on all fronts. The Roman Catholic authority decided that the Augustinian Order to which Luther belonged would first address the theses. In turn, the Augustinians decided that Luther's Ninety-Five Theses would be dealt with at a convention in Heidelberg in April 1518. Despite warnings from friends who were afraid for his safety, Luther decided to attend.

On April 11, 1518, Luther traveled with another Augustinian to Würzburg; he then joined with other Augustinians from Erfurt and traveled the one hundred miles to Heidelberg. At the convention, Luther's "new theology" was a hot issue of debate. For his part, Luther did not focus on the damages of indulgences but on how sinful human beings can still receive God's grace and forgiveness through faith in God alone. Among those who attended, Martin Bucer—who was a student at that time but later became Strasbourg's leading reformer—spoke very highly of Luther, whose "answers, so brief, so wise, and drawn from scripture easily turned all his hearers into admirers."[54]

The Hearing before Cardinal Cajetan in Augsburg

After he had returned from Heidelberg, Luther resumed his lectures at the university. On August 7, 1518, he received a letter that summoned him to Rome on suspicion of heresy. Sensing that this might lead to his death, Luther contacted Spalatin, who was his liaison with Freder-

---

54 Martin Bucer to Beatus Rhenanus, May 1, 1518. Quoted in Ibid., 70.

ick. He pleaded that the hearing be held in the Holy Roman Empire but not in Rome. He also informed Spalatin that the reputation of the university was at stake, hoping that this would move Frederick to fully support him.

As it turned out, the overall political atmosphere in the Holy Roman Empire worked in Luther's favor. Emperor Maximilian I needed Frederick's support for his grandson, Charles V, to succeed him.[55] In addition, the Turkish tax that Rome had imposed was promoting resentment within the empire, whose inhabitants worried that their money was going outside of the empire.[56] And so, Frederick persuaded the emperor to support Luther's petition. Rome's legate, Cardinal Cajetan, was also involved in negotiations. It was finally agreed that the hearing would be held in Augsburg.

In late September, Luther set out for the city. After twelve days of travel, he arrived in Augsburg on October 7, 1518. Frederick had appointed two of his advisors to accompany Luther. They prevented Luther from even meeting Cardinal Cajetan until the emperor had granted him safe conduct.[57] Since there was no Augustinian monastery in Augsburg, Luther stayed in a small cell on the first floor of the Carmelite cloister.

Four days later, Luther and Cajetan met at last. Cajetan had planned the meeting carefully; he played the caring father, who only wished to set his son on the right path. At the meeting, they discussed Luther's issues with the papal authority and indulgences. Luther refused to recant his opinions unless the Scripture could prove that he was wrong. The meeting necessarily failed. When Luther came to the second meeting accompanied by Staupitz, he promised to answer for his opinions in writing. So, on the third day, he appeared with a lengthy written document. In this document, he concluded, "As long as these Scripture passages stand, I cannot do otherwise, for I know that one must obey God rather than men…I do not want to be compelled to affirm something contrary to my conscience."[58]

---

55 Brecht, *Martin Luther*, 265–66.
56 Ibid., 263–65.
57 Ibid., 268.
58 Quoted in Roper, *Martin Luther*, 116.

At the end of the third meeting, Cajetan lost his patience. He sent Luther away, saying, "Either recant or do not show your face again."[59] He demanded that Staupitz convince Luther to recant. Staupitz kindly refused, stating that it was Cajetan's task to do so, not his.[60] Later that day, Staupitz heard rumors that the head of the Augustinian Order had requested Luther's presence in Rome, so he quickly released Luther from his Augustinian vows. Staupitz proved a valuable mentor to Luther at this time. On one occasion in Augsburg, he encouraged Luther thus: "You should bear in mind, brother, that you began this in the name of our Lord Jesus Christ."[61]

While waiting in Augsburg, Luther compiled his *Appellation to the Pope*. At the same time, his friends begged him to leave the city, as he could be taken to Rome at any moment. Late on the night of October 20, concealed in his monastic habit, Luther followed a single bodyguard, climbed over the city wall, and left for home.[62] The next day, his address to the pope was posted on the cathedral door.

Leipzig Disputation

Luther returned to Wittenberg on October 31, 1518—exactly one year after he posted the Ninety-Five Theses. However, he was now in despair. Anticipating a sentence of heresy, he indicated in a letter to Spalatin that he was ready "to go away as Abraham went, not yet knowing where but most sure of the way because God is everywhere."[63] He even organized a farewell dinner. It was not until he received word that Frederick wanted him to stay and continue to teach that Luther finally reconsidered.[64]

As 1519 began, the Holy Roman Emperor, Maximilian I, passed away. Two possible candidates came forward to replace him: Charles V of Spain and Francis I of France. Pope Leo did not support either

---

59 Hendrix, *Martin Luther*, 74.
60 Brecht, *Martin Luther*, 273.
61 Luther, *Luther's Works*, 48:191; Brecht, *Martin Luther*, 258.
62 Brecht, *Martin Luther*, 276.
63 Luther, *Luther's Works*, 48:94.
64 Hendrix, *Martin Luther*, 75.

one of them, as he feared that either would become a real threat to the papacy if they gained control of the Holy Roman Empire.[65] Therefore, the pope started to court Frederick the Wise to his side. Luther's heresy trial stalled. This was just as well, since Luther was now involved in a debate. Having read the Ninety-Five Theses, John Eck—a professor of holy scripture at the university in Ingolstadt—had declared that he would challenge Luther directly. He was well educated in humanism. He understood not only Latin, but Greek and Hebrew too. And, most importantly, he also knew how to use the printing press to promote his views. Luther willingly accepted Eck's challenge, and together, they decided that their debate would take place in Leipzig.[66]

Luther and his colleagues, including Andreas Karlstadt and Melanchthon, arrived in Leipzig on June 24. The disputation began on June 27, with a ceremonial service at St Thomas Church. After the opening ceremony, the two parties moved to an enormous room in Pleissenburg Fortress, where the debate was going to take place. It lasted about two weeks, during which both Luther and Karlstadt participated.

At first, Luther was surprised that the debate did not focus on indulgences. In fact, papal authority became the main focal point.[67] Eck argued that if Scripture had authority over papal superiority, then it was Jesus's saying, "you are Peter, and on this rock I will build my church" (Matthew 16:18) that gave divine authority to Peter and his successors. Luther opposed Eck's opinion, pointing out that the Eastern churches had never accepted the pope's authority. He provided a different interpretation of the Scripture, one in which "the rock" is Peter's *faith*, not Peter the person.[68] He even pointed out that no scriptural evidence could prove that Peter ever visited or lived in Rome. Incidentally, the debate also focused on such issues as sin and human nature.

While no official winner was ever declared, Eck's rhetorical skills had a clear edge over Luther's.[69] Eck was proud of what he had done at the debate, and he continued his campaign against Luther. Luther,

---

65 Brecht, *Martin Luther*, 288.
66 Ibid., 316–18.
67 Hendrix, *Martin Luther*, 79.
68 Ibid., 80.
69 Ibid.

on the other hand, was disappointed that the debate had not gone as planned. Be that as it may, the disputation gained Luther wider support among elite humanists and led to a gradual increase of interest in his writings.[70] The books Luther wrote were bestsellers in that time. The three pamphlets on his view of sacraments were printed in around 150 editions in 1519 alone. By 1520, more than 250,000 copies of his writings were in circulation.[71] His growing popularity is seen in the fact that the sales of his writings from 1518 to 1525 exceeded the next seventeen most prolific authors together.[72]

***

In the travel section that follows, I will introduce you to just two places: the Bavarian city of Augsburg, and a city known for its music today—Leipzig. In Augsburg, we will visit St Anne's Church, which was part of the cloister where Luther stayed, as well as the site where Luther met with Cardinal Cajetan. In Leipzig, we will visit St Thomas Church and the site of Pleissenburg Fortress (now the town hall), where the opening service and then the Leipzig Disputation took place respectively. Finally, we will visit other sites related to Luther's Reformation, including the University Church of St Paul and St Nicholas Church.

---

70 Ibid., 81.
71 Ibid.
72 Roper, *Martin Luther*, 142.

Travel: Augsburg and Leipzig

AUGSBURG

Located in the Bavaria region and dating back to the time of the Romans, Augsburg is one of Germany's oldest cities. It was a free imperial city for more than five hundred years, since 1276. In 1518, Martin Luther met Cardinal Cajetan in Augsburg, where he refused to renounce his beliefs. The Augsburg Confession—an important Lutheran confession—was declared at the chapel of the Episcopal Palace in 1530, though Luther was not present at that time.

The town hall of Augsburg
© Guido Radig / CC BY-SA 3.0.

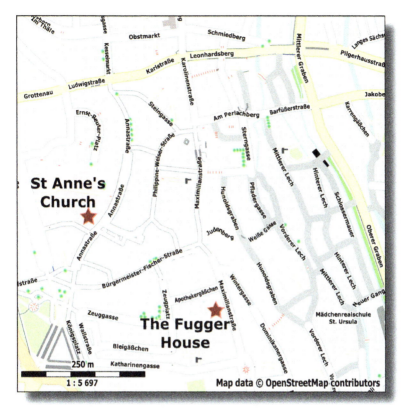

Map of Augsburg

The Fugger House (*Fuggerhäuser*)

Luther and Cardinal Cajetan met at the Fugger House in the old town of Augsburg. The Fuggers—a family of bankers who also commissioned the building of the Fugger Chapel in St Anne's Church—built it in the early sixteenth century. They also lent money to Albert of Mainz so that he could pay Rome for the title of archbishop. To repay his debts, Albert of Mainz promoted the selling of indulgences. The Fugger House was destroyed during World War II but rebuilt in 1951.

49

The Fugger House
© Alois Wüst / CC BY-SA 3.0.

St Anne's Church

Built in the fourteenth century, St Anne's Church is one of the earliest examples of Renaissance architecture. It was originally part of the Carmelite monastery. The Goldsmith Chapel and the Fugger Chapel were added to the church in 1420 and 1509 respectively. Luther stayed here in October 1518, during his meeting with the pope's legate, Cardinal Cajetan. The church's interior, with its colorful frescoes and devotional paintings, is an absolute gem to visit.

Today, St Anne's includes a small museum called Luther Staircase (*Lutherstiege*), which illuminates Luther's stay in Augsburg and his goings-on during Augsburg's Reformation. The museum includes the room where Lu-

The square in front of St Anne's Church
© Vitold Muratov / CC BY-SA 3.0.

ther stayed. It was here that he wrote his long defense reaffirming the authority of the Scripture over papal authority. The museum also displays the papal bull that was sent to Luther when he refused to recant, as well as other important Lutheran manuscripts and artifacts.

Interior of St Anne's Church
© JD / CC BY-SA 2.0.

LEIPZIG

Located about one hundred miles southwest of Berlin, Leipzig was an important trade city in medieval times. Today, the city is known for its music. Renowned German composers Johann Sebastian Bach and Felix Mendelssohn both spent a considerable amount of time in Leipzig. It also played an important role in the reunification of Germany. The Peaceful Revolution demonstration in 1989 was the result of a weekly prayer meeting, and it ultimately helped to topple the Communist regime.

A view of Leipzig
© Johannes Kazah / CC BY-SA 3.0.

Map of Leipzig

City History Museum (*Stadtgeschichtliches*)

This Renaissance-style building, which housed the town hall in 1556, now houses the City History Museum that exhibits Leipzig's history from prehistoric to modern times. Among its vast collections are artifacts from the Reformation including the Luther Chalice, Cranach the Elder's paintings of reformers, and Katharina von Bora's wedding ring. The ring was presented to Katharina at the time of her betrothal to Luther. It not only contains a ruby—a symbol of exalted love—but also has deep religious meaning: it features a crucified Jesus surrounded by various instruments of torture that were used at the crucifixion (the spear, the rod of reeds of the flagellation, the leaf of hyssop, the three nails, and the dice with which the soldiers cast lots). The inside of the band contains the couple's initials and their wedding date, June 13, 1525.

The old town hall, Leipzig
Photograph by the author

Pleissenburg Fortress (the new town hall)

Pleissenburg Fortress was where the famous Leipzig Disputation took place in 1519, when Luther debated the issue of papal authority with prominent Catholic theologian John Eck. The fortress from Luther's time no longer exists; the foundation became the town hall in 1905.

The new town hall, Leipzig
© Appaloosa / CC BY-SA 3.0.

St Thomas Church (*Thomaskirche*)

Dating back to the twelfth century, St Thomas Church is best known as the church where Johann Sebastian Bach served from 1723 to 1750. Bach's remains are buried here, in front of the altar. Over the centuries, St Thomas Church has gone through several reconstructions. The present structure, in the Late-Gothic style, was completed in 1496.

It was here that a ceremonial service took place in advance of the Leipzig Disputation. The cantor composed a special twelve-part Mass for the choir to sing at this service. Twenty years later, on Pentecost Sunday, Luther led the first public Protestant service here. A plaque was installed inside the church to commemorate this momentous occasion.

St Thomas Church with Bach Monument in front
Photograph by the author

54

*Plaque commemorating the introduction of
the Reformation in 1539*
Photograph by the author

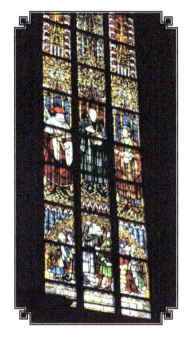

*Stained-glass window depicting
Luther (center), Frederick the
Wise (left), and Philipp Mel-
anchthon (right)*
Photograph by the author

The stained-glass window set above the entrance to the church was installed in the nineteenth century. It depicts Luther between Frederick the Wise and Philipp Melanchthon. The lower part of the stained-glass window depicts Luther nailing the Ninety-Five Theses to the wooden door of Castle Church in Wittenberg.

Thüringer Hof

When Thüringer Hof was erected in 1466, it was designated as a hostel for students of the town's university. Luther's friend, Dr. Heinrich Schmiedeberg, owned it. During Luther's visits to Leipzig, he often stayed at the tavern. Unfortunately, the original building was destroyed in World War II. What you see today is a reconstruction from the 1990s.

Auerbachs Keller

Auerbachs Keller was a historic restaurant and wine bar even in Luther's day. It was established by Heinrich Stromer von Auerbach, a professor of medicine at Leipzig University, in the sixteenth century. Attracted to Luther's ideology, Professor von Auerbach invited Luther to his place during the famous Leipzig Disputation in 1519. A few years later, when Luther was on his way from Wartburg to Wittenberg, he issued another invitation. A room at the restaurant, known as the Luther Room, illustrates these historical events. A few centuries later, German poet Johann Wolfgang von Goethe spent some time here too. Indeed, it was here that he found the inspiration for a famous scene in his play, *Faust*.

The sculpture depicting the scene in Faust in front of Auerbachs Keller
© Dr. Avishai Teicher / CC BY-SA 4.0.

University Church of St Paul (*Paulinerkirche*)

Built in 1231, the University Church of St Paul was initially the Dominican Order's monastery. Johann Tetzel, the preacher who promoted the selling of indulgences, was buried here. On August 12, 1545, Luther led the consecration service that turned the monastery church into the Protestant University Church of St Paul. Although the original church suffered little damage during World War II, it was demolished by the Communist regime in 1968. The new church was completed only recently, its architecture inspired by the design of the original building.

The newly built University Church of St Paul
Photograph by the author

St Nicholas Church (*Nikolaikirche*)

Built in the twelfth century and named after the patron saint of trade, St Nicholas Church is Leipzig's oldest church. The church contains a Gothic-style pulpit known as Luther's Pulpit. It was also where the Peaceful Revolution originated in the 1980s, when what started as an afternoon prayer meeting became a movement that went on to topple the Communist regime.

Interior of St Nicholas Church
Photograph by the author

Chapter 6: Diet of Worms and Wartburg Castle

Tracts in 1520

Following the Leipzig Disputation, the attacks on Luther intensified. John Eck traveled around the country, publicly criticizing Luther. He also renewed his attack on Luther through his writings. On June 15, 1520, Luther received the papal edict *Exsurge Domine* ("Arise, O Lord"). The edict depicted Luther as a wild boar and his supporters as foxes destroying the vineyard of the Lord. Luther was threatened with excommunication unless he recanted his earlier positions. It was under this enormous pressure that Luther continued his writings in 1520. After all, his quill was his best weapon against any threats. Three notable writings from 1520 include *To the Christian Nobility of the German Nation*, *On the Babylonian Captivity of the Church*, and *On the Freedom of a Christian*.

Published in mid-August 1520, the tract *To the Christian Nobility of the German Nation* was intended to appeal to the emperor and the nobility of Germany. In this work, Luther argued that since the church was too corrupt to reform itself, the lay authorities would have to take the initiative. He writes, "If that is not a brothel above all imaginable brothels, then I do not know what brothels are."[73]

Written in Latin and completed in October 1520, *On the Babylonian Captivity of the Church* was much more radical than any of Luther's earlier works. The title suggested that Christians are like the Israelites, who were exiled in Babylon after the fall of Jerusalem and the destruction of the Temple. Luther equated Rome to Babylon and the pope to the

---

73 Luther, *Luther's Works*, 44:154.

antichrist. In this treatise, Luther argued that there are only two sacraments, not seven, since only baptism and communion are attested by the Scriptures. He also redefined the sacrament as "God's promise of salvation." This promise is not obtained through any works, but only through faith. He said, "the sacraments…are not fulfilled when they are taking place, but when they are being believed."[74]

Published in November 1520, *On the Freedom of a Christian* described how Christians should live by the gospel. Luther argued that human beings have two natures, the inner and the outer. Authentic Christian living, as he described it, is "where faith is truly active through love, that is, it finds expression in works of the freest service, cheerfully and lovingly done, with which we willingly serve one another without hope of reward."[75] Luther further emphasized the need for ordinary Christians to make judgments instead of blindly following what others have said. He asserted, "Everyone can pass a safe judgment on all works and laws and make a trustworthy distinction between them and know who are the blind and ignorant pastors and who are the good and true."[76]

On December 10, 1520, the deadline that Luther had been given to recant, he walked out through the Elster Gate to the Chapel of the Holy Cross after his morning lecture. Accompanied by his students, he burned the papal decretals, the canon law, and the edict. Luther was not only denouncing papal authority; he was denouncing the entire tradition of canonical law. In his letter to Staupitz, he wrote, "I have burned the books of the pope and the bull, at first with trembling and praying; but now I am more pleased with this than with any other action of my life for [these books] are worse than I had thought."[77]

The Diet of Worms

The edict that excommunicated Luther came from Rome on January 3, 1521. Those who protected him were also declared heretics. For Frederick, an imperial diet would be his last resort to try to ease the

74 Roper, *Martin Luther*, 164.
75 Luther, *Luther's Works*, 31:365.
76 Ibid., 31:370.
77 Quoted in Roper, *Martin Luther*, 169.

situation. He tried to persuade Emperor Charles V to arrange a hearing for Luther.[78]

When the Diet of Worms began on January 27, 1521, Charles V was still undecided.[79] While there were delegates who simply wanted Luther to be condemned, there were also some who supported having Luther heard. To the young emperor, the risk of not having Luther heard was too high. In March 1521, Charles V finally summoned Luther to the diet. This was not a friendly gesture, as he also ordered Luther's books be collected and burned.[80] He was determined to have Luther recant when he arrived in Worms. On April 2, 1521, just four days after Luther received the summons, he set out on the journey, accompanied by friends and supporters.

It was a journey of more than three hundred miles, and Luther and his friends stopped en route to visit Erfurt, where Luther was warmly welcomed by the crowds. It was a Saturday, but Luther remembered it so well that he later described it as "my Palm Sunday."[81] Many people lined up to see him. He preached at the university, and a reception was organized afterward. On the morning of April 16, after two weeks of travel, Luther and his friends arrived in Worms. An imperial herald led the procession to the city. Luther was taken to the quadrangle of the Order of the Knights of the St John, where he would stay.

The next morning, Luther was informed that he would appear before Emperor Charles V and his court at the bishop's residence late that afternoon. Eager crowds climbed to the rooftops to see. Luther, in a simple black-belted cassock, was escorted through the side entrance into a room where the emperor, the electors, their advisors, and delegates waited. In the room, a pile of his books was placed on the bench in front of him. The emperor's spokesman, John von der Ecken, presented Luther with two questions in Latin and German. Pointing to Luther's books on the bench, Ecken asked whether the books were written by him. He then asked Luther whether he would recant or not.

---

78 Brecht, *Martin Luther*, 449.
79 For a thorough discussion, see: Ibid., 450–58.
80 Ibid., 463.
81 Hendrix, *Martin Luther*, 102.

Luther did not answer instantly. In that shocked pause, Frederick's advisor, Jerome Schurff, demanded that the titles of the books be read out loud.[82] This gave Luther some time to react. He admitted that the books were his writings, and he asked for time to think over his answer to the second question. He was given one day, though Eck warned that a recantation was expected.

The next afternoon, Luther was led to the bishop's residence again. He was obligated to wait until six o'clock, as the emperor and the delegates had other business to attend to.[83] He was then brought to a larger room, so crowded that many delegates had to stand. The two questions were repeated to him. Luther replied first in Latin and then in German, and each answer lasted ten to fifteen minutes. Explaining that there was no reason for him to recant everything, he grouped his books into three categories: books that explained Christian faith and life; books that criticized the papal authority; and books that responded to those who attacked him. Regarding the third category, he admitted that he might have been harsh with his language, but that he was not a saint. He then referred to the word of Jesus, "I did not come to bring peace but a sword" (Matthew 10:34).

While Charles V and his advisors discussed privately what to do next, Eck demanded that Luther answer whether he would recant. Luther stood firm and gave this historical reply: "Unless I am convinced otherwise by evidence from Scripture or incontestable arguments, I remain bound by the Scripture I have put forward. As long as my conscience is captive to the Word of God, I neither can nor will recant, since it is neither safe nor right to act against conscience. God help me. Amen."[84]

After Luther refused to recant, he was dismissed. On the evening of that same day, Charles V and his advisors made up their decision to proceed with excommunication. In a letter, Charles V wrote: "We are not able to depart from the example of our ancestors in defending the ancient faith and giving aid to the Roman See. Therefore, we shall

---

82 Brecht, *Martin Luther*, 469.
83 Ibid., 472.
84 Luther, *Luther's Works*, 32:112-13.

pursue Martin himself and his adherents with excommunication and use other methods available for their liquidation."[85]

Despite his decision, Charles V asked a committee to seek Luther's recantation once more. After some negotiation, Luther insisted that his writings be judged only by the Scripture. After this attempt failed, Frederick's advisors recommended that Luther leave Worms immediately upon extended safe conduct. Luther and his companions departed the city on April 26, 1521. Charles V's official Edict of Worms was made public a month later. While this edict remained in effect throughout Luther's lifetime, it was never enforced in Saxony. For the young emperor, it was too much of a political risk to offend Frederick the Wise.[86]

Wartburg Castle

On his way home from Worms, Luther stopped to visit several places. After visiting his relatives in Möhra, he was "kidnapped" per Frederick the Wise's prearranged plan to protect him. He was taken to Wartburg Castle in Eisenach. Instead of dressing in the cloth of a monk, he wore the clothes of a knight. He also let his tonsure grow. His appearance changed so much that many people could not recognize him when he appeared again. During the time Luther remained in the castle, his mobility was confined. He still corresponded with his friends and colleagues, but it was not the same as living in Wittenberg. As he later described it, this castle was "his Patmos."[87] Thus, Luther compared his experience to that of John the Apostle, who wrote the book of Revelation while imprisoned on the island of Patmos.

By October, it had become clear that returning to Wittenberg would not be an option in the near future, so Luther found momentum in a new project. He began translating the New Testament from Greek into German. Although his was not the first German translation of the New Testament, it had a profound effect. Luther's translation reshaped

---

85 Hendrix, *Martin Luther*, 107.
86 Brecht, *Martin Luther*, 492.
87 Hendrix, *Martin Luther*, 110.

the German language by unifying the different dialects.[88] This New Testament translation was eventually printed in September 1522, six months after Luther returned to Wittenberg. Because it was published in September, it was also described as the September Testament.

***

In the travel section, we will visit the ancient imperial city of Worms. The site where Luther stood firm before the imperial court is now a city park. We will also explore one of the largest Luther monuments, and a few other sites related to Luther.

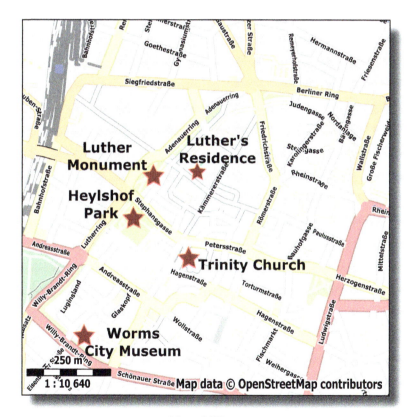

Map of Worms

---

88 Roper, *Martin Luther*, 207.

Travel: Worms

Situated on the Upper Rhine, Worms is an ancient city that dates to Roman times. It has been a Roman Catholic bishopric city since the seventh century. In the Middle Ages, the city received free imperial city status and reported directly to the Holy Roman Emperor. For this reason, Worms was one of the places where imperial diets were held.

Luther's Residence (*Johanniterhof*)

On Hardtgasse Street is a building with a plaque on the wall commemorating Luther's stay here. Because he was advised not to leave his residence, Luther was perhaps the most visited person during the Diet of Worms.

Luther Monument (*Lutherdenkmal*)

Designed and constructed by Ernst Rietschel and his pupil, Donndorf, the Luther Monument was inaugurated in 1868. The center statue shows Martin Luther's appearance before the Diet of Worms. With a Bible in hand, Luther is surrounded by forerunners of the Reformation, including John Wycliffe, Peter Waldo, Girolamo Savonarola, and Jan Hus; his protector, Frederick the Wise; his supporter, Philipp I, Landgrave of Hesse; and his colleagues, Johannes Reuchlin and Philipp Melanchthon. Reliefs and medallions depict important stages of the Reformation. Seated women symbolize the towns of Speyer, Augsburg, and Magdeburg.

Luther Monument in Worms
© Vitold Muratov / CC BY-SA 3.0.

Worms City Museum (*Museum der Stadt Worms*)

Located in St Andrew's Collegiate Church, Worms City Museum exhibits the history of the city. There is a special room dedicated to Luther and the Diet of Worms in 1521. A copy of the Luther Bible of 1521 (his German translation of the New Testament) with handwritten annotations is exhibited here. Another important artifact is the bust of Luther that artist Ernst Rietschel originally designed for the Luther Monument.

Worms City Museum, formerly St Andrew's Collegiate Church
© Altera Levatur / CC BY-SA 4.0.

Heylshof Park (*Heylshofgarten*)

Once the site of the imperial palace, Heylshof Park is located on the north side of the Cathedral of Worms. It was here that Luther made his famous speech on April 18, 1521. A simple plaque near the cathedral marks the spot where Luther stood. The inscription reads, "*Hier stand vor kaiser und reich Martin Luther* 1521." In English, that translates to, "Here stood Martin Luther before the empire and the nation 1521."

Museum in Heyshof Park
© Heidas / CC BY-SA 3.0.

Trinity Church (*Dreifaltigkeitskirche*)

Trinity Church was dedicated by the city as a Reformation memorial church in the eighteenth century. This Baroque-style church was damaged heavily during World War II. After the war, the city decided to preserve the outer façade and renovate the interior completely. Inside the church, to one side of the organ, a mosaic on the wall depicts Luther's appearance at the Diet of Worms.

*Interior of Trinity Church, with the mosaic of Luther's appearance at the Diet
on the wall*

Chapter 7: Back to Wittenberg

While Martin Luther was in Wartburg Castle, reform efforts were underway in Wittenberg including the abolition of monastic vows and private masses, and reforming of the sacraments.[89] Luther was satisfied with many reforms that were underway. However, a few instances of reform caused disturbances towards the end of 1521 and the beginning of 1522.[90] Despite concerns from Frederick's advisors, Luther's colleague Karlstadt stepped up and led a service on Christmas Day. He celebrated Communion in German and had the laity distribute the host and chalice. A few days later, some visitors from nearby Zwickau arrived in Wittenberg and lodged with Karlstadt. They supported lay preaching and rejected infant baptism. In early January, 1522, Gabriel Zwilling initiated a destruction of icons, statues, and other sacred items. Luther was concerned that the efforts to reform might become too radical.

On January 24, 1522, the town of Wittenberg finally adopted reforms. Upon hearing the news, Luther decided that it was time to return to Wittenberg. Despite Frederick's wish that he stay in Wartburg Castle, Luther did not comply. In a letter to Frederick, he gave three reasons: first, the congregation at Wittenberg wanted him to return. Second, the power of the devil had already infiltrated the sheepfold; since he was entrusted by God to minister the people, he must return. Third, he was concerned about a rebellion.[91]

---

89 Hendrix, *Martin Luther*, 121.
90 Ibid., 124.
91 Luther, *Luther's Works*, 48:389-90.

After eleven months away, Luther returned to Wittenberg on March 6, 1522. On March 9, he began preaching a series of sermons, later known as the *Invocavit* or Wittenberg Sermons.[92] He reminded the congregation of the importance of Christian values, and he distinguished changes that were absolute from those that were optional, as he thought it best to give time and space to those who were not ready to change. His return signified a change in leadership of the Reformation in Wittenberg. Compared to Karlstadt's, Luther's reformation efforts were moderate.

Not only was Luther assuming a position of reformation leadership in Wittenberg, but he was also involved in the challenging task of reforming churches outside of Wittenberg. He was involved in preaching, recommending pastors, reorganizing church finances, and composing materials for worship.[93] This created a very busy work schedule. As a result, during the first few years after he returned from Wartburg Castle, he spent less time on polemics but more corresponding with pastors outside of Wittenberg.

Marriage to Katharina von Bora

In April 1523, a group of Cistercian nuns—who had been convinced by Reformation teachings against monasticism—escaped their convent near Leipzig and arrived in Wittenberg. These women came from the upper nobility, but their families were unable to welcome them back for fear of violating Catholic canon law. They had hidden inside empty barrels on a wholesale grocery wagon in a prearranged escape. They were escorted to Wittenberg and warmly welcomed by the town. A few of the nuns stayed in Cranach the Elder's home. Luther praised the escape in a public letter to Leonhard Koppe, a city councillor and merchant at Torgau who had helped the nuns escape. In the letter, Luther encouraged the nuns' families to let their daughters return home.[94] Luther believed that chastity was God's gift, and that no one—not even if vows had been taken—was guaranteed to receive it. Luther was also involved in matchmaking, to discourage malicious gossip.[95]

---

92 Ibid., 51:70-100.
93 Hendrix, *Martin Luther*, 147.
94 Ibid., 143.
95 Roper, *Martin Luther*, 274.

In 1525, two nuns who lived in Cranach's residence were married, one to a nobleman and the other to a man who worked in Cranach's pharmacy. The third nun who lived in Cranach's residence was Katharina von Bora. She first fell in love with Jerome Baumgartner, a former student in Wittenberg who came from a prominent Nuremberg family. Katharina waited for a proposal from him, but it never came. Luther then tried to arrange a marriage between Katharina and another pastor, Caspar Glatz. Katharina rejected that proposal. She told Luther's friend, Nikolaus von Amsdorf, that she would marry only him or Luther. Luther gladly accepted her as his wife. In a letter to Amsdorf, he said, "I feel neither passionate love nor burning for my spouse, but I cherish her."[96]

On June 13, 1525, Luther and Katharina were married. After the wedding, Katharina moved from Cranach's house to the cloister, which had been given to the couple as a wedding gift from Elector John (Frederick having passed away a month before). Despite the fact that Katharina had no dowry and Luther's salary was small, she knew how to run a household well. She not only tracked all of the incomes and expenses but also grew vegetables and made necessary repairs to the home.[97] She and Luther had six children.

The Peasants' War

In the fall of 1524, about eight months before Luther's wedding, a series of local rebellions in southwest Germany had gradually coalesced into a major uprising known as the Peasants' War. These peasants were not satisfied with their present situation of serfdom, and they took up arms against their landlords. They merged with radical reformers such as Thomas Müntzer, who thought that the reformation process was not going swiftly enough. The peasants' leaders formed armies and drafted a constitution based on their vision of an egalitarian society. Although they achieved some initial success, they were quickly defeated by the professional army in the Battle of Frankenhausen in May 1525.

Luther was not in favor of rebellion. In *Admonition to Peace*—which

---

96 Luther, *Luther's Works*, 49:116-18.
97 Hendrix, *Martin Luther*, 167.

had been published before the Battle of Frankenhausen—even though he condemned both the lords who oppressed their subjects and those peasants who wanted a rebellion, he condoned the slaughter of the peasants. Referring to the killing, he wrote, "If anyone thinks this is too harsh, remember that rebellion is intolerable and that the destruction of the world is to be expected every hour."[98] This was one instance in which Luther received wide criticism in his time and from later historians.

Theological Controversy over the Lord's Supper

In late 1524, a major division surfaced among the reformers concerning the understanding of the Lord's Supper. Like other reformers in his time, Luther rejected the Catholic doctrine of transubstantiation, the conversion of the bread and wine to the actual body and blood of Christ at the consecration. Reformers such as Karlstadt and Huldrych Zwingli held the view that believing in the physical presence of Christ's body was superstitious. For them, the sacrament was a reminder of the Last Supper Jesus had with his disciples. On the other hand, and despite his rejection of transubstantiation, Luther still believed in the actual presence of Christ (as he interpreted Jesus's words of institution literally). He did not think that the sacrament was a commemorative event. For Luther, the Lord's Supper was not reserved for the righteous; it was for all sinners. 1524 marked only the beginning of the controversy over the Lord's Supper. It would continue for the rest of Luther's lifetime.

***

In the travel section that follows, we will visit the remaining sites in the quiet town of Wittenberg, including the former Augustinian cloister, where Luther lived both before and after his wedding; the town church where Luther preached thousands of sermons; the location where he burned the papal bulls that threatened his excommunication; and the house where Philipp Melanchthon lived.

---

98 Luther, *Luther's Works*, 46:54-55.

Travel: Wittenberg Part 2

Luther House (*Lutherhaus*)

Located near the east end of Wittenberg, this house was Luther's residence in Wittenberg. It was originally built as an Augustinian cloister. As the Reformation movement progressed, the cloister gradually emptied. When Luther married Katharina in 1525, the elector gave the Augustinian cloister to the couple as a wedding present. Today, it is a museum of Luther's Reformation including an excellent display of manuscripts—which includes the printed copy of the Ninety-Five Theses—paintings, the original pulpit from the Town Church of St Mary's, a gown that is believed to be Luther's, and other items related to the Reformation.

Exterior of the Luther House (to the bottom right is the door that Katharina gave to Luther as a birthday gift in 1540)
Photograph by the author

Luther Room (Lutherstube)

Luther enjoyed the company of his friends, colleagues, and students. He would often invite them to his house for supper. This is the room where Luther and his guests would gather after supper for conversation. These conversations were recorded and later published as Luther's *Table Talk*.

Luther Room (Lutherstube)
Photograph by the author

Statue of Katharina

In the middle of the courtyard is a statue of Luther's wife, Katharina. This statue was completed in 1999 to celebrate her five hundredth birthday. It shows Katharina stepping through a doorway, signifying her leaving the convent and walking toward a new life.

Statue of Katharina von Bora
Photograph by the author

The Cellar

The cellar illuminates how Katharina ran the household in Luther's day. In order to manage a large household including their children, several nephews and nieces, ten to twenty students, and visitors, Katharina turned part of the Augustinian cloister into boarding houses for students. She also bought farmlands and livestock.

The cellar
Photograph by the author

Town Church of St Mary's (*Stadtkirche St Marien*)

Built in the late twelfth century, the Town Church of St Mary's is the oldest building in Wittenberg. It is often called the "Mother Church of Reformation" as the first Protestant service was held here on Christmas Day, 1521. Johannes Bugenhagen, a colleague of Luther's, was the first minister chosen after the church adopted Protestantism.

Luther saw this church, where he witnessed many important family events, as his home church. This was where his children were baptized and where he delivered more than two thousand sermons. It was also in this church that Luther's most famous hymn, "A Mighty Fortress Is Our God," was first sung.

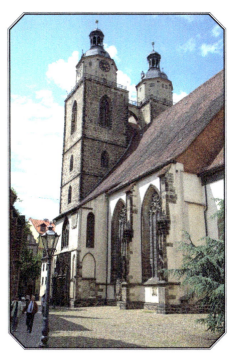

Town Church of St Mary's
© Paul T. McCain / CC BY-SA 2.5.

The Reformation Altarpiece

The Reformation Altarpiece is the must-see art piece at St Mary's, completed one year after Luther's death. It was a collaborative work by Lucas Cranach the Elder, Lucas Cranach the Younger, and their school. The top-center image is a reenactment of the Last Supper; it shows the major Reformation leaders enjoying fellowship with each other. The rounded table emphasizes the equality of Christians—that no one is above anyone else. In the scene, Cranach the Younger is passing the cup to Luther. The top-left image, wherein Melanchthon (who was not an ordained priest) is baptizing a baby, depicts the theme of baptism. The top-right panel features Bugenhagen holding the key to heaven. The man on Bugenhagen's left is earnestly confessing his sins before God and kneeling to receive the key. The man on Bugenhagen's right is trying to buy his way into heaven, and his hands are tied. Bugenha-

75

gen holds the key behind the man's back to signify that the ticket to heaven can never be purchased. The bottom painting shows Luther at the pulpit, preaching the Word of God to a congregation that includes Katharina, who listens carefully. Between the crowd and Luther is the crucifixion of Jesus. That image helps to convey the message that the Word is the true gospel of Jesus Christ.

The Reformation Altarpiece (in front) and the baptismal font (left)
© Gunnar Bach Pedersen, via Wikimedia Commons.

Baptismal Font

Cast by Hermann Vischer in Nuremberg in 1457, the baptismal font is the oldest fixture in St Mary's. Luther's children were baptized here. A noteworthy feature is the tube that extends from the basin directly down to the ground, signifying the washing away of sin. Around the lower legs of the font, the evil demons' efforts to reach the baby are thwarted by the saints who are guarding the baby.

Luther Oak Tree (*Die Luthereiche*)

To commemorate the three hundredth anniversary of the Augsburg Confession, the Luther Oak Tree was planted in 1830, on the spot where Luther burned the papal bull *Exsurge Domine*.

The plaque that commemorates the burning of the papal bull in 1520
Photographs by the author

Luther Oak Tree, planted in 1830
Photographs by the author

Melanchthon House (*Melanchthonhaus*)

Melanchthon House
Photograph by the author

Philipp Melanchthon (1497–1560), Luther's colleague and right-hand man, came to Wittenberg when he was twenty-one. He was a brilliant professor with extensive knowledge of the Greek language. In order to keep Melanchthon in Wittenberg, Frederick the Wise arranged for him to marry Katharina Krapp, the mayor's daughter, on November 25, 1520. In 1536, the elector and the university decided to give him a gift of a new house to be built on his original home site on the street of Collegienstraße. After the house was completed in 1539, Melanchthon and his family lived there until his death in 1560.

Melanchthon House is now a museum that portrays Melanchthon's life from the perspective of his nine-year-old daughter. Many of Melanchthon's original works are displayed there.

Luther Monument in Market Square (*Marktplatz*)

Market Square is located in the center of the old town. In Luther's time, it was used as an all-purpose space for events such as tournaments or executions, or as a hunting ground for the electorate. In front of the square is a beautifully decorated town hall (*Rathaus*).

The Luther Monument, erected in 1821, is located to the right of Market Square. To the left of the Luther Monument is a statue of Philipp Melanchthon. Its location signifies his importance to Luther.

The Luther Monument in Market Square
Photograph by the author

Luther Garden

Established in the first decade of the twenty-first century, the Luther garden is located on the grounds of the former Fortress of Wittenberg. The center of this garden features a path in the shape of a Luther rose, a symbol for Lutheranism. This garden features hundreds of trees. Each tree in the Luther Garden has a sister tree somewhere else in the world, planted in Christian communities to show ecumenism.

Luther Garden
© Ktmd, via Wikimedia Commons.

Chapter 8: Organizing the Church

Establishing Reforms

In May 1525, about a month before Luther's wedding, Frederick the Wise died on a hunting trip. His brother John assumed his responsibilities as elector. Unlike Frederick, who had only allowed some reforms here and there, John supported Luther wholeheartedly. On October 31, 1525, eight years after the publication of his Ninety-Five Theses, Luther sent John a proposal that consisted of three requests.[99]

The first was for John to secure the future of Wittenberg's university, as its financial stability was top priority. In response, John transferred two-thirds of the endowment funds from All Saints' Chapter—the institution that managed Frederick's relic collection—to the university and the final one-third to Castle Church.

Luther's second request was for the authorization of a new order of service in German. This new order of service, called the *German Mass*, was finally completed by Luther.[100] It was not the first German order of service, as such liturgies were already available in places like Strasbourg or Nuremberg. However, Luther intended for the order of service to be adaptable to German culture. Perhaps this was why it became so popular. He completed the chants of the words of institution and the traditional biblical readings but left the other compositions to professional musicians. The town church of Wittenberg adopted this

---

99 Ibid., 49:130-37.
100 For the translation of the complete *German Mass*, see Ibid., 53:51-90.

reform after Christmas of 1525, and the *German Mass* went into publication in January 1526.

Luther's third request was for permission to establish rules and regulations for the maintenance of parishes around the region. This request could not be granted immediately because the Edict of Worms of 1521—which had made Luther, John, and Luther's other supporters outlaws—was still in effect. It was not until the Diet of Speyer that the way was cleared. At that diet, which Archduke Ferdinand (Charles V's brother) chaired, it was decided that political unity was more important than religious unity. The empire needed troops and money to defend Hungary and Austria from the Turks, regardless of whether the territories were inclined to religious reform. The diet's decision meant that John could start authorizing visitations to parishes in Saxony.

But before visitations could take place, guidelines had to be established. These guidelines, known as the *Instruction of the Visitors for the Parish Pastors in Electoral Saxony* (and often called the *Instruction*) were prepared by Spalatin and Melanchthon.[101] Luther was called to Torgau to review these guidelines at the end of September and again at the end of November in 1527. The *Instruction* offered theological principles as well as practical suggestions for the organization of churches. It was published in late March 1528, more than ten years after the Ninety-Five Theses. It was a long stretch, but Luther had patiently waited for the fruit to ripen as he sowed the seeds of reformation through his writings. In retrospect, his moderate approach resulted in the establishment of Protestant churches in Germany, whereas Thomas Müntzer's radical reform through the Peasants' War ended in failure.

On June 7, 1526, Luther and Katharina's first child, John, was born. The following year, their first daughter, Elisabeth, was born on December 10. Unfortunately, she lived for only eight months. The death of his daughter left Luther in grief. In a letter to Hausmann, Luther articulated his heartache: "My little daughter, Elisabeth, has expired. I marvel that my soul is so sick…I never imagined that parents could love their children so much!"[102]

---

101 See Ibid., 40:263-320.
102 Ibid., 49:203.

In late 1528 and early 1529, Luther participated in parish visitations in Saxony. His visit was cut short when illness forced him to stop participating in March. This actually gave him more time to work on his catechisms: the *Small Catechism*, for ordinary people and pastors, and the *Large Catechism*, mainly for clergy. These catechisms were based on the *Little Prayer Book* that Luther had published in 1522.

Besides writing many tracts and treatises, Luther was also involved in producing hymns. He knew that music had the special capability to instill faith into the hearts and minds of the people. He wrote twenty-eight hymns from 1523 to 1530 and eight more after 1530. "A Mighty Fortress Is Our God" was likely composed sometime between 1527 and 1529. Also known as the "Battle Hymn of Reformation," its lyrics contain common themes from Luther's time. Using the notion of fortification in Wittenberg, Luther reminded the faithful that God is the ultimate fortress against any calamities or devils that one might face. It was through reliance in God that one would prevail and achieve ultimate victory.

Marburg Colloquy

In 1529, the empire's diet was held in Speyer. No longer interested in allowing towns and territories to decide their own religious affairs, Archduke Ferdinand, Charles V's brother who chaired the diet, reinstated the Edict of Worms. The nobles who supported reform quickly wrote a formal protest (from which the term *Protestant* comes), but it was rejected. Fearing that the emperor might organize a military campaign against the Protestant territories, Philip of Hesse, a Protestant nobleman, invited Protestant leaders to Marburg to discuss a joint Protestant statement. In mid-September, Luther, Melanchthon, Justus Jonas, and a few others journeyed from Wittenberg and arrived in Marburg on the morning of September 30.

The colloquy was held from October 1 to 4, 1529. Most of the discussions were among the four theologians in residence: Luther, Melanchthon, Zwingli, and Johannes Oecolampadius.[103] Toward the end

---

103 Hendrix, *Martin Luther*, 231.

of the conference, a draft document called the *Marburg Articles* was prepared to be signed. It contained fifteen paragraphs. The attendees agreed on every one of its points—except on whether the true body and blood of Christ were present during the Lord's Supper. They decided to add a statement vowing that "each side should show Christian love to the other side insofar as conscience will permit, and both sides should diligently pray to almighty God that through his Spirit he might confirm us in the right understanding."[104] The debate over the Lord's Supper continued to deter them from forming a unified theological front.

Augsburg Confession

In the spring of 1530, a new diet was to begin at Augsburg. Emperor Charles V was determined to defend the empire from Turkish invasion as well as resolve the conflict between Catholics and Protestants. Upon receiving the news, Elector John invited Luther, Jonas, Melanchthon, and others to accompany him. The group traveled from Torgau and made a stop at the town of Coburg, the southernmost town in Saxony.[105] Since the edict that had outlawed Luther was still in effect, it was decided that Luther would wait at Coburg while the elector and the others continued on to Augsburg.

As one of the major agendas of the diet was to discuss religious matters within the empire, some Lutheran[106] nobility thought that a united front was necessary to present their confession of faith, known as the *Augsburg Confession*, to the emperor. Melanchthon was asked to draft this important document. After he completed the draft, it was sent to Coburg for Luther to review. Luther was generally satisfied with Melanchthon's work but felt that it did not go far enough to completely reject the papacy and its authority.[107] The final version of the confession was signed by the political officials of Lutheran cities and territories—including Nuremberg, Reutlingen, Electoral Saxony,

---

104 Luther, *Luther's Works*, 38:88-89.
105 While Coburg belongs to Bavaria today, it was part of Saxony in Luther's time.
106 The term *Lutheran* will now be used to refer to the Protestants who sided with Luther or were in general agreement with his theological views.
107 Luther, *Luther's Works*, 49:297-98.

Hesse, Lüneburg, Brandenburg-Ansbach, and Anhalt—on June 23 and presented to Charles V two days afterward. The Catholics responded quickly with a refutation known as *The Confutation* on August 3, 1530.

The rest of August saw Catholics and the Lutherans negotiating to reach an agreement. However, they stalled over many issues, such as the Lord's Supper, monastic vows, and abolishing private masses. Neither side was willing to compromise. Eventually, the emperor gathered the delegates and announced that the *Augsburg Confession* was refuted on September 22.

Elector John, Melanchthon, and the others left Augsburg and arrived in Coburg on October 1. Luther joined them, and they all left Coburg on October 4. What they thought would be a short trip ended six months later. While waiting in Coburg, Luther had spent his time preaching as well as corresponding with his colleagues in Augsburg. In June 1530, he had also written his commentary on Psalm 118 entitled *The Beautiful Confitemini* ("the beautiful confession of one's faith").[108] Psalm 118:17 was his personal motto, as it announced, "I will not die but live, and will proclaim what the Lord has done."

In Coburg, Luther suffered a deeply difficult time following the news of his father's death. In a letter to Melanchthon, Luther reflected, "Even though it comforts me that my father, strong in faith in Christ, fell gently asleep, yet sadness of heart and the memory of the most loving dealings with him have shaken me in the innermost parts of my being, so that seldom if ever have I despised death as much as I do now."[109]

Schmalkaldic League

The Edict of Augsburg led to the forming of the *Schmalkaldic* League, an alliance of mostly Lutheran princes designed to defend against Catholic attack. Around this time, Luther's view of resistance changed somewhat. He still opposed Christians taking up their swords to resist authority; however, he also viewed the princes' resistance against

---

108 For Luther's commentary on Psalm 118, see Ibid., 14:41-106.
109 Ibid., 49:318.

any external pressure and attack as permissible. This was likely due to the fact that the Protestant princes were defending themselves against Catholic forces. In Luther's January 1531 letter to Wenzel Linck, he wrote, "If princes as princes are permitted to resist the emperor, let it be a matter of their judgment and their conscience. Such resistance is certainly not permitted to a Christian, who has died to the world."[110]

The German Bible of 1534

After returning from Coburg, Luther resumed work on his translation of the German Bible—a joint effort by a team of translators. The New Testament was based on Luther's translation from when he had been in Wartburg Castle, and the Old Testament was translated by a group of scholars. In September 1534, their translated Bible was finally published. Even after the Bible was published, Luther continued to revise the translation. The New Testament was revised six times before 1534, and the entire work was revised three times before his death in 1546.

***

In the travel section, we will visit the beautiful towns of Coburg and Torgau, the latter of which features a splendid collection of Renaissance and Late-Gothic buildings. I will introduce you to the magnificent fortress in Coburg, where Luther spent time in 1530, and the Gothic church where he preached seven times. I will also introduce the castle church in Torgau, which Luther consecrated as the First Protestant Church, as well as the elegant town church where Luther's wife was buried.

---

110 Quoted in Hendrix, *Martin Luther*, chap. 14.

Travel: Coburg and Torgau

COBURG

Situated between the Upper Main Valley to the south and the Thuringian Forest to the north, Coburg is now known as the "Road of Castles" in honor of the many castles and palaces in and around the town. Coburg was the birthplace of Queen Victoria's husband, Prince Albert.

Map of Coburg

Town hall of Coburg, Germany
© Störfix / CC BY-SA 3.0.

During the Diet of Augsburg in 1530, Luther stayed in the town for five and a half months while his colleagues and Elector John attended the diet. He first lived in a townhouse in Coburg but was soon moved to the Veste Coburg Fortress for his safety. During his stay, messengers went between Coburg and Augsburg to keep him informed of news from the diet. Although communication was often thin during these months, Luther was able to correspond with Melanchthon and discuss the newly drafted confession.

The town house where Luther first stayed
© Störfix / CC BY-SA 3.0.

Veste Coburg Fortress

Veste Coburg Fortress sits atop a hill. It is one of the largest and best-preserved castles in Germany, dating back to the eleventh century. During his stay, Luther worked on his translation of the Old Testament in addition to writing sermons, tracts, and numerous commentaries. He also received important visitors, such as Martin Bucer, who was the Protestant leader in Strasbourg.

Veste Coburg Fortress
© Störfix / CC BY-SA 3.0.

Today, the castle is open to the public and includes a museum that houses the collections of artwork, arms, and armor of the ducal family. It also features Luther's former study and living room. The exhibit includes a portrait of Luther with a Bible in his hands, painted by Cranach the Elder in 1540, as well as the seventeenth century painting, *The Reading of the Augsburg Confession*, depicting that event at the Diet of Augsburg. A Luther memorial stands on the stone wall of the castle; its inscription is Luther's motto, taken from Psalm 118:17: "I will not die but live, and will proclaim what the Lord has done."

Luther Monument with inscription
of Psalm 118:17
© Störfix, Lizenz / CC BY-SA 3.0.

St Moriz Church (*Morizkirche*)

Dating back to the fourteenth century, St Moriz Church is the oldest church in the town. It houses the family tomb of the dukes of Coburg. During his residency in Coburg, Luther preached at this church seven times; he even gave the sermon on Easter Saturday, the day after he arrived.

St Moriz Church
© Tilman2007 / CC BY-SA 3.0.

TORGAU

Located on the banks of the Elbe, about thirty miles southeast of Wittenberg, Torgau is filled with around five hundred beautiful Renaissance and Late-Gothic buildings. It was already a beautiful place in Luther's time; even he declared that the buildings here were more beautiful than those in any other town. Today, Torgau is best known as the site where American and Soviet forces met in April 1945.

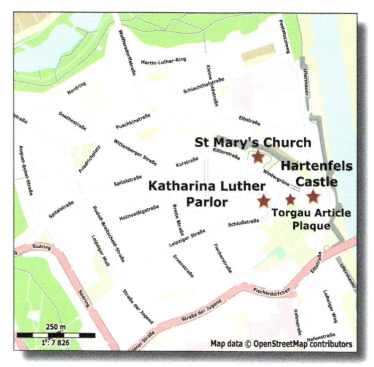

Map of Torgau

In Luther's time, the town was the primary residence of Elector John and the electoral seat of Saxony. Luther often traveled here to conduct the business of the court and the church. In fact, he came here more than sixty times throughout his life. Here, Luther was involved in the discussion of many important documents, including the first Protestant hymnbook in 1524, the *Instruction of the Visitors for the Parish Pastors in Electoral Saxony* in 1527, the *Torgau Articles* in 1530, and the *Schmalkaldic Articles* in 1536.

Town of Torgau
© Zeppelubil Th. Haft / CC BY-SA 3.0.

Castle Church (*Schlosskirche*) in Hartenfels Castle

Located in Torgau's Hartenfels Castle, Castle Church was the first Protestant Church built after 1517. Its interior was simple, as Luther had envisioned. The motifs on the pulpit and the painting of the interior were done by Lucas Cranach the Elder. On October 5, 1544, Luther came to inaugurate the church. Johann Walters, one of the founders of the Protestant vocal music style, composed the music for this event.

Interior of Castle Church
© Andreas Praefcke / CC BY-SA 3.0.

Sculpture of Luther in Hartenfels Castle

Located in the main courtyard of Hartenfels Castle, the residence of Saxon electors, is a beautiful spiral staircase known as the *Grosse Wendelstein* ("the Impossible Staircase"). It was constructed without a central supporting column. The entry to the staircase is painted and ornamented with stone carvings illustrating important historical scenes from the Reformation and of Saxony. The oldest sculpture of Luther is located at the top of the staircase.

Hartenfels Castle, with the spiral staircase in the center
© Radler59 / CC BY-SA 4.0.

St Mary's Church (*Marienkirche*)

Though dating back to the twelfth century, St Mary's Church was rebuilt in the second half of the fifteenth century. The Late-Gothic church—the oldest church in town—dominates the Torgau skyline. Luther used to preach here.

St Mary's Church
© A. Köppl, Gleiritsch / CC BY-SA 3.0.

St Mary's Church is also the burial site of Katharina von Bora. After Luther's death, she continued to live in Wittenberg. In 1552, an epidemic struck Wittenberg and caused the university to relocate. Katharina and her two youngest children, Paul and Margaret, left Wittenberg and headed to Torgau. On their way, the horses shied and Katharina fell from the wagon. She remained in bed in Torgau for three months and eventually died there on December 20, 1552. Her gravestone is decorated with a painting of her standing and holding a Bible. At the top two corners of the painting, the Luther and von Bora coats of arms appear in bas-relief.

Tombstone of Katharina von Bora
© Clemensfranz / CC BY-SA 3.0.

Plaque of Torgau Articles

In March 1530, Luther, Melanchthon, Jonas, and Bugenhagen gathered to create a document to present to the emperor at the Diet of Augsburg. In the Superintendency of Torgau, they drafted the *Torgau Articles*. Today, a plaque that commemorates this event is attached to the wall of the house.

Plaque that commemorates the Torgau Articles
© Concord / CC BY-SA 3.0.

Katharina Luther Parlor

This beautiful Renaissance building is where Katharina died on December 20, 1552. Torgau was not only her final resting place but also where she had her "rebirth": it is where she first stayed after fleeing the convent in April 1523. Today, the building has become a museum dedicated to her. It presents the story of her life as well as artifacts from her time.

Chapter 9: Final Years

For the rest of the 1530s, Luther witnessed important events including the signing of the *Wittenberg Concord* on May 29, 1536. In early 1537, the Schmalkaldic League convened to discuss the future of the Protestant faith as well as the antinomian controversy with people like Agricola, who argued that the Old Testament law should not be preached or taught. During this time in Wittenberg, Luther continued to lecture, preach, and ordain new Lutheran pastors. Meanwhile, Lutheran strength continued to grow. In 1539, following the death of Duke George, Duke Henry (prince of the other part of Saxony and George's successor) turned the region into Lutheran territory.

In 1537, Luther's health began to deteriorate; he suffered kidney stones and did not feel well for months at a time.[111] Indeed, health issues continued to bother him into the 1540s. On September 20, 1542, Luther's third eldest child, Magdalena, died. He grieved profoundly. At Magdalena's funeral, Luther spoke to those who attended: "Do not be sorrowful; I have sent a saint to heaven. In fact, I have now sent two of them."[112] His first daughter, Elisabeth, had preceded Magdalena in death by fourteen years.

In April 1544, an epidemic struck Wittenberg and all four of Luther's surviving children were ill. Luther reported his family's illnesses to a friend, saying, "I have lived long enough if one may call it living."[113] On January 17, 1546, about a month before his death, Luther lost sight in one of his eyes. As he was over sixty, it appeared that age had taken its toll.

---

111 Ibid., chap. 17.
112 Luther, *Luther's Works*, 54:433.
113 Ibid., 50:245-46.

On January 22, 1546, Luther set out on his final journey to Eisleben, the town where he was born. He needed to settle a dispute regarding his family business. He took with him his three sons: Hans, who was nearly twenty; Martin, who was nearly fifteen; and Paul, aged thirteen. When they reached Halle, winter conditions forced Luther to stay there and wait until the passage was cleared.[114] On the way to Eisleben, Luther became very dizzy. He blamed his collapse in the wagon on the work of the devil.[115] Once they arrived, Luther stayed in the house of Dr. Drachstedt, a family friend in the mining business, and negotiations began. Luther's illness made him feel like returning home, but the meeting dragged on for weeks.

While in Eisleben, Luther preached four times at St Andrew's Church. He also ordained two pastors on February 14, 1546. His daily routine included a prayer around eight o'clock in the evening; he stood by the window and prayed intently. The negotiation finally reached a partial agreement, but Luther was not well enough to participate on February 17. Later that evening, while eating his supper, perhaps aware that his life was coming to an end, he reflected with his friends on whether the dead can recognize one another after life. When he went to his rooms to pray that evening, he fell ill with chest pains and a chill, so he napped for an hour around nine.

After he woke up, he walked into another room. As he crossed the threshold, he spoke the words, "Into your hand I commend my spirit. You have redeemed me, God of truth."[116] Returning to his room, he shook each person's hand and wished them a good night. Justin Jonas; Luther's two sons, Martin and Paul; and his servants stayed beside him. His pain did not go away. Around one o'clock in the morning, he said to Jonas, humorously, "I think I will stay here at Eisleben where I was born and baptized." He walked into his privy and repeated the same words he had said before.[117]

---

114 Hendrix, *Martin Luther*, 283.
115 Roper, *Martin Luther*, chap. 19.
116 Ibid.
117 Ibid.

Luther was rubbed and given warm cushions to help ease his pain. He then prayed, saying, "You revealed to me Your dear Son Jesus Christ, in whom I believe, whom I have preached and proclaimed [and] whom the accursed Pope and all the godless shame, persecute and blaspheme against."[118] He continued, "I am traveling hence, I will relinquish my spirit." He finally repeated three times in Latin, "Father, into your hands I commend my spirit, You have redeemed me, God of Truth."

Jonas and Michael Coelius asked him, "Reverend Father, will you die faithful to Christ and to the doctrine you have preached?" Luther replied with a firm "yes." After a quarter of an hour, he died in peace.[119]

Luther's body was taken back through Halle to Wittenberg. While it was in Halle, Luther's death masks and casts of his hands were made. On February 22, Luther's body arrived in Wittenberg. A long procession gathered to take the coffin through the gate at the east end of the town. The procession then passed through the university, past Luther's residence, and entered Castle Church at the west end of town. At Luther's funeral, Bugenhagen gave the sermon and Melanchthon delivered a Latin oration. Melanchthon presented Luther as a prophet—just like Old Testament prophet Elijah, who had led the people of Israel. He made the remark that "a few people who should not be despised have complained that Luther was sharper than we could bear. I will not quarrel with them or with Luther's defenders. I respond rather with that which Erasmus often said: 'Because the maladies were so severe, God has given our age an abrasive physician.'"[120]

***

In the final travel section, we will first visit the historic town of Halle and the Market Church with its gorgeous towers. We will then visit the quiet town of Eisleben, where Luther was born and later passed away. I will introduce you to Luther's birthplace and place of death; St Andrew's Church, where he gave his final sermons; and the Church of St Peter and St Paul, where he was baptized.

118 Ibid., 401.
119 Ibid., chap. 19.
120 Quoted in Hendrix, *Martin Luther*, 278.

Travel: Halle and Eisleben

HALLE (SAALE)

L ocated in the southern part of the German state of Saxony-Anhalt, about twenty-two miles from Leipzig, Halle is now an important educational and economic center. Its history dates to the ninth
century. In Luther's time, Archbishop Albert of Mainz—who heavily
promoted indulgences—lived in Moritzburg, a fortresslike residence
in Halle. His collection of relics is housed in the Dominican cloister
next to Moritzburg. Luther visited the city and preached at the Market
Church several times.

The Market Square in Halle
© OmiTs / CC BY-SA 3.0.

Map of Halle's old town

Market Church (*Marktkirche*)

Located in the Market Square of Halle, Market Church was built in the sixteenth century on the former site of two church buildings. The church's four towers and the red tower of the city hall create the most notable landmark of Halle. For this reason, Halle is also known as the "City of the Five Towers." The church's library, the *Marienbibliothek*, is probably the largest Protestant church library in Germany.

Justus Jonas introduced Reformation to the city and served as Market Church's pastor in the 1540s. Luther preached three times in this church; he even gave two sermons in January 1546, shortly before his death. The original pulpit from which he preached is still preserved.

Market Church in Halle
© OmiTs / CC BY-SA 3.0.

When Luther died at Eisleben on February 18, 1546, casts of his face and hands were made, and they can be viewed in a small room inside. The cast was later altered to disguise the effects of a stroke on one of his eyelids.

In 1685, Germany's famous composer, George Friedrich Handel, was baptized at Market Church. The original baptismal font can be seen inside. A statue of Handel stands in front of Market Square to commemorate his talent and his connection with the city.

EISLEBEN

Located in Saxony-Anhalt, Germany, Eisleben is a historic town that dates back to at least the tenth century. Until the eighteenth century, it belonged to the counts of Mansfeld. This town played an important role in Luther's life; it was both his birthplace (November 10, 1483) and the place of his death (February 18, 1546). Every year, a festival to celebrate Luther's birthday is held from October 31 to November 11.

Old town of Eisleben
© Dguendel / CC BY-SA 3.0.

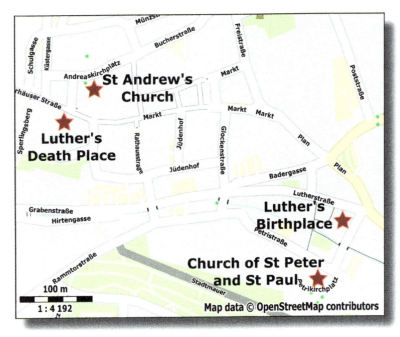

Map of Eisleben

Luther's Birthplace (*Martin Luthers Geburtshaus*)

The exhibition title "That is where I'm from—Martin Luther and Eisleben" captures the theme of the museum in Luther's birthplace. The original house no longer exists; it was destroyed by a major fire in 1689. In 1693, the house was reconstructed and turned into a public museum, making it one of the world's oldest heritage tourism sites. Since then, the house has been renovated several times.

The museum illuminates Luther's family origins, from the mining business of his father, Hans Luder, to Luther's baptism. It also exhibits artifacts from Luther's time. Above the front door is a large relief with a portrait of Luther, the Luther Rose, and an inscription that translates, "God's Word and Luther's teaching will never pass away. Dr. Martin Luther was born in this house in the year 1483 and was baptized in the Church of St Peter and St Paul."

Luther's Birthplace
© Jwaller / CC BY-SA 3.0.

St Andrew's Church (*Andreaskirche*)

Located in the historic old town of Eisleben, the two spires of St Andrew's Church have been the town's focal point for many centuries. St Andrew's is, in fact, the largest church in Eisleben, and Luther preached his final four sermons here. In his last sermon, he preached on Matthew 11:28, which reads, "Come to me, all you who are weary and burdened, and I will give you rest." This was a suitable message, as Luther labored to the end of his life and died only a few days later.

St Andrew's Church, Eisleben
© Andreas-Wettbewerb / CC BY-SA 3.0.

Inside the church is the original pulpit from which Luther preached, accessed by eleven narrow steps. The pulpit is still used on special occasions. In 1817, to celebrate the three hundredth anniversary of the Reformation, busts of Luther and Melanchthon were commissioned; they were completed by Berlin sculptor Johann Gottfried Schadow.

The Church of St Peter and St Paul (*St-Petri-Pauli-Kirche*)

The Church of St Peter and St Paul was built between 1447 and 1513. This Gothic-style church was where Luther was baptized on November 11, 1483. The original baptismal font in which he was baptized still exists and can be seen in the middle of the chancel. The church's interior was renovated in 2010, uncovering both austerity and elegance. A new baptismal font, the Luther Font, was added at that time. The arches in the nave bear the marks of guild signs, family arms, and the Luther Rose.

Interior of St Peter and St Paul
© Rabanus Flavu via Wiki Commons.

Luther's Death House (*Martin Luthers Sterbehaus*)

Located opposite the Eisleben Market is the house where Luther supposedly died. The two-story house features a long side building and a spiral staircase. It was named Luther's Death House in 1726. In 1863, the Prussian government acquired it and established a memorial on site. From 2010 to 2013, a modern museum was added to the house. Today, the museum sheds light on Luther's final days and houses many historical relics, including period furniture and the original cloth that covered Luther's coffin. The exhibit also features works that explore Luther's thoughts on death and dying.

Luther's Death House
© Olaf Meister / CC BY-SA 3.0.

Bibliography

Brecht, Martin. *Martin Luther: His Road to Reformation, 1483-1521.* 1st pbk. ed. Minneapolis: Fortress Press, 1993.

Hendrix, Scott H. *Martin Luther: Visionary Reformer.* New Haven: Yale University Press, 2015.

Kolb, Robert, Irene Dingel, and Lubomir Batka, eds. *The Oxford Handbook of Martin Luther's Theology.* First edition. Oxford Handbooks. Oxford ; New York, NY: Oxford University Press, 2014.

Luther, Martin. *Luther's Works.* Edited by Helmut T Lehmann and Jaroslav Pelikan. Philadelphia; St. Louis, Mo.: Fortress Press ; Concordia Pub. House, 2002.

Meller, Harald, Siegfried Bräuer, Jutta Charlotte von Bloh, Landesausstellung Fundsache Luther - Archäologen auf den Spuren des Reformators, and Landesmuseum für Vorgeschichte, eds. *Fundsache Luther: Archäologen auf den Spuren des Reformators ; [Begleitband zur Landesausstellung "Fundsache Luther - Archäologen auf den Spuren des Reformators" im Landesmuseum für Vorgeschichte Halle (Saale) vom 31. Oktober 2008 bis 26. April 2009].* Stuttgart: Theiss, 2008.

Roper, Lyndal. *Martin Luther: Renegade and Prophet,* 2016.

"St. George's Church, Mansfeld." Accessed September 28, 2016. http://www.welterbe-luther.de/en/extension-application/st-georges-church-mansfeld.

Copyright and Credits

About the Book

Martin Luther, the renowned sixteenth-century reformer, was a man who fully devoted his life to God. His deep faith led him to nail his Ninety-Five Theses to a church door on October 31, 1517, protesting the corruption within the Roman Catholic Church. His trust in God's providence allowed him to stand firm in front of Holy Roman Emperor Charles V at the Diet of Worms in 1522, where he bravely refused to recant his views. His conviction that all German people should be allowed to read the living Word of God led him and other scholars to translate the Bible into German. It was Luther's determination that helped solidify the Reformation in Germany.

On this journey through the life and faith of Martin Luther, you will follow in his footsteps from his childhood in Mansfeld and adolescence in Eisenach; through his time in Erfurt, where he studied to become a monk; and finally, to his residence in Wittenberg, where he had a successful career as a professor. You will discover the disputations with which he was involved in Augsburg and Leipzig, what he accomplished at the Imperial Diet at Worms in 1522, why he was forced to hide in Wartburg Castle, and much more. Maps, photos, and historical backgrounds of each town will introduce you to the castles, the churches, and many other historical sites that were of special importance to Martin Luther throughout his lifetime.

CPSIA information can be obtained
at www.ICGtesting.com
Printed in the USA
LVOW05s1952170118
563079LV00027B/1300/P

9 780995 826632